thai *cooking*

Jackum Brown
consultant: Rachanee Boonthon

cooking

photography by Sandra Lane

hamlyn

First published in the U.K. in 1998 by Hamlyn
an imprint of Octopus Publishing Group Limited
2–4 Heron Quays
London E14 4JP

Copyright © 1998 Octopus Publishing Group
Limited

Distributed in the United States and Canada by
Sterling Publishing Co., Inc.
387 Park Avenue South
New York, NY 10016 - 8810

This U.S. edition copyright © 2000
Octopus Publishing Group Limited

ISBN 0 600 60094 7

Thai Cooking
Jackum Brown

Publishing Director: Laura Bamford
Editor: Anne Crane
Assistant Editor: Sharyn Conlan
Creative Director: Keith Martin
Senior Designer: Geoff Fennel
Photographer: Sandra Lane
Home Economist: Oona Van den Berg
Stylist: Mary Norden
Indexer: Hilary Bird
Production Controller: Bonnie Ashby

Americanized by: Barbara Horn

Produced by Toppan
Printed in China

Author's acknowledgements

I owe a great many thanks to Rachanee Boonthon for helping me create these
recipes, and for spending countless afternoons with me in her restaurant, the Thai
Café in Fortess Road, London NW5; Benjarmas and Kitisak Boonthon were also
very helpful. Thanks are due to David Brown, Gabrielle Mander, Nigel Fountain and
Monica Henriquez, without whom I could not possibly have managed.

Notes

All dishes serve 4 people, when served
as part of a Thai meal.

Eggs should be medium unless
otherwise stated. The USDA advises
that eggs should not be consumed raw.
This book contains dishes made with
raw or lightly cooked eggs. It is advisable
for more vulnerable people such as
pregnant and nursing mothers, invalids,
the elderly, babies, and young children to
avoid uncooked or lightly cooked dishes
made with eggs. Once prepared, these
dishes should be kept refrigerated and
used promptly.

Milk should be whole unless otherwise
stated.

Fresh herbs should be used unless
otherwise stated. If unavailable, use
dried herbs as an alternative and halve
the quantities stated.

This book includes dishes made with
nuts and nut derivatives. It is advisable
for those with known allergic reactions
to nuts and nut derivatives and those
who may be potentially vulnerable to
these allergies, such as pregnant and
nursing mothers, invalids, the elderly,
babies, and children to avoid dishes
made with nuts and nut oils. It is also
wise to check the labels of preprepared
ingredients for the possible inclusion of
nut derivatives.

Ovens should be preheated to the
specified temperature. If using a fan
assisted oven, follow the manufacturer's
instructions for adjusting the time and
temperature.

Thai cooks rarely seed chiles (the seeds
and surrounding membrane are the
hottest part). If you prefer a milder
flavor, remove the seeds before use.

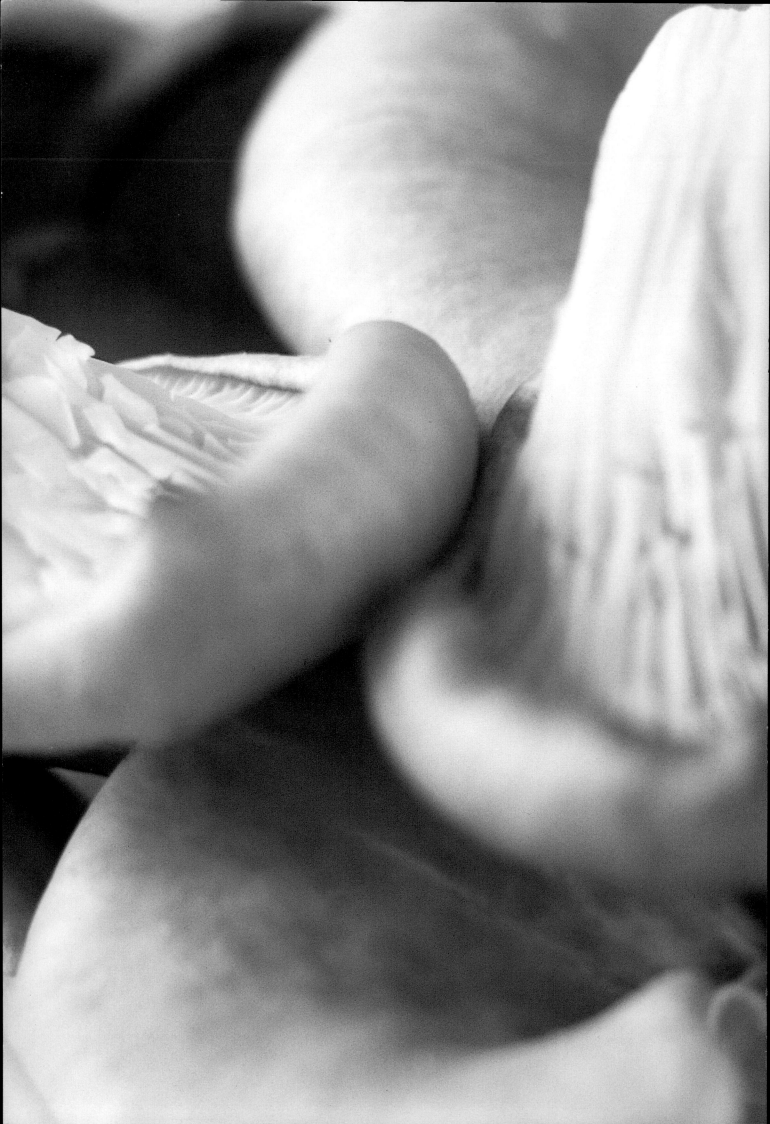

contents

Thailand is a beautiful and fertile country that produces some of the best food in the world. There is no doubting the importance of good food to Thai people. From the moment you set foot in the country your senses are assailed from all sides with the smell of delicious barbecue chicken and dried squid, the sound of pestles thudding into mortars and cleavers chopping vegetables, and the sight of exotic fruits loaded onto stalls, while out of the corner of your eye you see a huge whoosh of flame reaching up around a wok and the cook laughing at your surprise.

Food markets in Thailand are an absolute joy to explore: the produce is so fresh and so exotic, and there are always scores of mysterious items for sale that you have never seen before. Thailand is still overwhelmingly an agricultural country and its major natural resource is its agricultural potential. Although the agricultural sector's contribution to Thailand's gross national product has declined considerably in the last 40 years due to the huge growth in manufacturing output, it still employs two-thirds of the labor force and directly supports 60 percent of the population.

Introduction

Thailand is one of the only countries in Asia to export more food than it imports, and has been the world's largest exporter of rice since 1981. Most Thai rice is produced under natural rain-fed conditions, using little fertilizer, so production depends on prevailing weather conditions. As the world's weather patterns become more and more erratic, the late or non-appearance of monsoons or the extreme conditions of drought, flooding, and hurricanes produced by El Niño, for example, may prove disastrous for all of us and not just for the citizens of the countries that are directly affected.

The good thing about countries like Thailand, where the agriculture is still largely unintensive, is the fabulous quality of what is produced. Problems arise where intensive farming for profit is undertaken too hurriedly. For example, in Thailand cassava (tapioca), which is a subsistence crop in most countries that grow it, is almost all exported to Europe, mainly as cattle food pellets. However, production is declining, as it makes heavy demands on soil nutrients, and soil erosion and exhaustion are being reported. Similarly, overfishing has depleted inshore fish stocks, although aquaculture and the development of canning and freezing facilities have greatly expanded the export of shrimp and squid to Japan, the United States, and Europe.

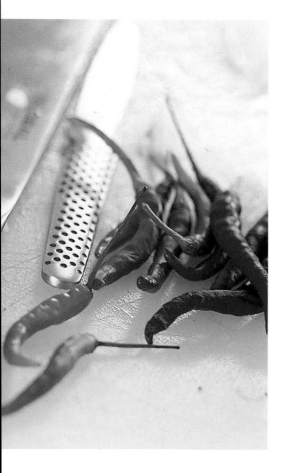

The Thai diet is a very healthy one: plenty of fresh vegetables and fruit, good quality rice, noodles, and small amounts of meat and fish. Dairy products are virtually unused by the majority of Thai people, and cattle raising is on a small scale. In fact, there has been something of a beef shortage since 1990, forcing a steep rise in beef imports. The climate and topography of Thailand are not very suitable for cattle—there are far more pigs, chickens, and ducks, and this is reflected in the recipes.

There are about 60 million people living in Thailand, the vast majority of whom are of the Thai ethnic group and are Therevada Buddhists. Buddhism was adopted in the thirteenth century, and Buddhist teaching has given rise to a reluctance to take the life of any creature. Historically, wealthy Thais would try to gain merit by buying a whole catch of fish and returning it to the sea. Nowadays people can buy little songbirds in bamboo cages and set them free for the same purpose. Butchers are rarely ethnic Thais, but fishermen are another matter.

Fish is very important in the Thai diet and always has been. The whole country is crossed by rivers and natural waterways, so freshwater fish and shellfish are readily available in places where fresh fish from the sea is unobtainable. Much fish of all types is dried, salted, or turned into fish paste or fish sauce—all highly nutritious and essential providers of protein. If you ask how fishing—a very popular activity—squares with Buddhism, you will

Left: chiles; Above: stir-frying noodles; Above right: stir-fried squid with basil (see page 86)

often receive a big smile along with the expression "mai pen rai" (no problem). Ask again and the most essentially Thai explanation is that fish stupidly get caught in traps and have to be rescued from drowning! Fishermen don't kill them, but if the fish then die, why shouldn't they be eaten?

Thailand's cuisine has been influenced by various countries and the Thais have refined all these influences to form a unique style of their own: highly spiced with sharply contrasting flavors and textures. There are clean citrus tastes from kaffir limes, lime leaves, and lemon grass; sourness from tamarind; sweetness from coconut milk and palm sugar; and spiciness from distinctive ginger, galangal, krachai, essential garlic, and all-pervading chiles. Chiles were brought to Thailand in the early sixteenth century by the Portuguese. Until then, hot black pepper was used, but chiles loved the climate in Thailand and the Thais loved chiles. Cardamom came from India via Burma, cilantro and cumin arrived from the Middle East, tapioca from Central America, and tomatoes from South America via Europe.

A Thai meal generally consists of a number of different dishes plus a large bowl of rice. There might be a soup—either in a large bowl that everyone can dip into, or small individual bowls—a curry, something steamed or fried, a salad, some noodles, various sauces and pickled vegetables, and fresh fruit to finish the meal. All these dishes will appear on the table at the same time and you put a mound of rice on your plate, followed by a little of one of the other dishes. Thais do not put everything on their plates at once and eat it all together. They like to appreciate all the different tastes and textures separately. Thais use either their fingers or a fork and spoon to eat with, except in the case of noodles, where chopsticks are used—a sign of Chinese influence on Thai cuisine.

Unless it is a special occasion, you will not find a dessert being served, other than fruit. There are a large number of Thai desserts or sweetmeats, and a great many of them involve egg yolks and sugar—another legacy of the Portuguese. Some of them take a long time to make and involve a number of stages. I sometimes wonder whether they aren't more highly prized because of the length of time involved in their making rather than for the tastes themselves. Generally speaking, most Thais lead hard, busy lives and do not spend hours cooking complicated food. They go to the market and find whatever looks good that day, take it home, and rustle up something delicious in a very short space of time. While we were cooking the recipes that appear in this book, my friend and consultant Rachanee suddenly became quite worried: "Everyone will say, 'Oh, it's too quick, it's too easy, it can't be right,'" but that is one of the joys of cooking Thai-style: as long as you have the basic ingredients, you can make a delicious meal quickly and without much trouble.

Thai kitchens are very simple compared to Western kitchens, so you will probably already have most of the equipment you need to cook Thai food. You really do need a wok, however, and I suggest a wooden-handled one; some of the cheaper woks have metal handles and you can give yourself a bad burn if you aren't careful. The shape of the wok allows its entire surface to heat up, with the hottest part at the center. When you stir-fry, it is best to heat the wok, add a little oil, swirl it around, and get it good and hot before you add your first ingredients. Think about what you are cooking, and put in the ingredients that require the most cooking first, leaving delicate leaves or beansprouts to the end. Don't be afraid of tossing the food around in the wok; you need to keep moving it from the center to the sides and back again. The whole experience of Thai cooking is very much hands-on—there is lots of chopping and pounding and tearing and mincing. Most Thais do not have ovens, so they do not employ the sort of long, slow casserole cooking or roasting that we go in for.

You will also need a steamer, ideally either a stainless steel one, which you will find very useful in your everyday cooking too, or a bamboo steamer of the kind you can find in an oriental shop. A mortar and pestle is useful for blending chiles, garlic, onions, and other spices and achieving an authentic texture. A cleaver is a very useful item for chopping vegetables, chopping through bones, peeling pineapples, and opening coconuts. A bamboo-handled wire basket can be used for blanching vegetables, plunging noodles into stock or boiling water for a few moments to cook, and for removing deep-fried food from the hot oil. A long-handled spatula, shaped rather like a shovel with a long handle, is ideal for moving the ingredients around while stir-frying.

Having said this, there are always alternatives. You could use a large skillet instead of a wok, rig up a colander over a large saucepan of water as a steamer—just put a lid over whatever you are steaming—I always cook rice this way. A slotted spoon can be used for removing deep-fried food from the oil and for stir-frying, as can wooden spoons. You can use a small food processor or coffee grinder instead of a mortar and pestle, although if you use the coffee grinder for its original purpose, make sure you clean it out thoroughly both before and after whizzing up your spices, or you might find yourself drinking chile-hot coffee with overtones of lime leaf and cilantro!

Thais do eat very, very hot food. Not every dish contains chiles, of course, but you would never have a Thai meal that wasn't hot in part. Some of the recipes in this book may be too hot for chile-beginners, so seed the chiles to tone down the heat. Be very careful when handling them: They contain an oil that is so strong it can even make your skin sting, so wash your hands really thoroughly, scrubbing under the nails, after you have touched them, and don't touch your eyes, nose, or mouth until you have done this. Generally speaking, the smaller the chile, the hotter it is; and when they are young and green they tend to be hotter than when they are mature and red or yellow. To seed them, hold the stem in one hand and, with the sharp point of a knife, split the chile from top to tip and

Below: bamboo steamers; Right: broiled beef with spicy sauce (see page 62); Far right: deep-fried sea bass (see page 80).

then scrape out the white seeds and ribs inside. With dried chiles, just take the stem end off and roll the chile around in your fingers to loosen the seeds, which will then fall out of the open end.

If you are thinking of really getting into cooking Thai food, I would recommend taking a trip to an oriental food store or supermarket. Here you will not only be able to buy everything you need, in both food and equipment terms, but do so very economically. Although most supermarkets and many small food shops carry some useful items, such as noodles, bamboo shoots, and soy sauce, they cannot compete with the real thing. For example, Thai jasmine or fragrant rice can be bought in 10- or 20-pound sacks, which will last a long time and is considerably cheaper than buying it in 1-pound boxes or bags.

Cooking Thai-style may seem a little alarming to begin with—so many small amounts of different things go into each dish, and somehow a number of different dishes have to be ready to eat at more or less the same time. The answer is to choose your menu carefully. Rice can be reheated very easily in a steamer. Curries can also be cooked in advance and reheated. Soup can be cooked in a saucepan, leaving your wok free for deep-frying a fish or stir-frying, and salads can be prepared in advance and finished at the last moment. As with any other form of cooking, the more often you do it, the easier it becomes, until you find you can turn out inexpensive, nutritious meals at the drop of a hat, and your family and friends will consider you a star. Whether or not you become addicted to Thai food, you will certainly know that you are eating healthily, and I am sure you will enjoy its scented and exotic flavors.

Jackson Brown

Basil Holy basil has purple stalks and smaller, darker leaves than sweet basil. In Thai cooking, it is used as commonly as the sweet basil we usually use, which is sweeter and which may be substituted.

Bamboo shoots The young, ivory-colored, conical-shaped shoots of edible bamboo plants are tender and slightly crunchy, and add texture and sweetness to many Asian dishes. Bamboo shoots are available canned, fresh, and sometimes vacuum-packed.

Bean sauce Black, yellow, and red bean sauces made from preserved soy beans are available in jars. Black beans are available in cans and bags, and should be rinsed and chopped before use. Unused beans and their liquid can be stored indefinitely if they are kept in a sealed container in the refrigerator. Bean sauce and beans can be bought from most supermarkets and oriental food shops.

Chiles There are so many different kinds of chile that it would be impossible to list them all. As a general rule, the smaller the chile, the fiercer the heat. Red chiles are slightly less fierce than green, since they become sweeter as they ripen. Most of the heat of chiles is contained in and around the seeds and the inner membrane. Thai cooks often include the seeds in cooking, but you may prefer to remove them for a milder flavor. Fresh orange and yellow chiles are often used in Thai cooking, for their pretty colors as much as anything else. You can occasionally buy them from specialist oriental shops and markets, but otherwise use whatever color you can get.

Chinese broccoli This is available fresh at oriental shops. It is quite like sprouting broccoli except that it is longer and thinner, with more stalk and less floret. The stalk is the most interesting part, and it is sliced and cooked in many different ways.

Cilantro This wonderful herb is an essential ingredient in Thai cooking. All of it is used— the leaves, stalks, and roots. You can store the roots in an airtight container in the refrigerator or in the freezer.

Coconut milk and cream These are widely available in cans, cartons, and blocks (which require added water). You can make coconut milk yourself from desiccated coconut: Place 2 cups desiccated coconut in a blender with 1⅓ cups hand-hot water; blend for 30 seconds,

Glossary

then strain the liquid through cheesecloth, squeezing it as dry as you can. This will produce thick coconut milk. If you return the coconut to the blender and repeat the process, then mix the two extractions, you will get a medium-thick coconut milk, suitable for most dishes. If you put this milk in the refrigerator, the "cream" will rise to the surface and can be taken off. Coconut milk lasts only 1–2 days, even in the refrigerator. If you are using coconut cream, stir it all the time while cooking because it curdles easily.

Curry paste Ready-made pastes are available in jars, or you can make your own (see pages 18–19). They freeze perfectly.

Eggplant Asian eggplants are either long and thin and pink, small and round and pale green, or tiny and round and darker green. They are often available in large supermarkets and Asian and oriental food shops. If you substitute the large purple-black variety more commonly found, remember that they cook faster than the Asian varieties, so adjust your cooking times accordingly.

Egg roll wrappers White and flimsy, these are made from flour and water, and are usually square. Buy them ready-made, fresh or frozen in plastic bags, from oriental shops and some supermarkets. They are very fragile, so handle them gently, especially if they have been frozen. If you can't find the shape you need for a recipe, buy whatever you can and cut to the required shape. If egg roll wrappers prove hard to find, use phyllo pastry instead, and cut the sheets to size.

Left: fresh cilantro; Below: greater galangal (sometimes called Thai ginger); Right: gai choy (mustard cabbage).

Fish sauce (*nam pla*) Thais use fish sauce in a great many dishes. It is available in most large supermarkets and in oriental food shops.

Galangal This is a root similar to ginger, but the skin is thinner and slightly pink, and the taste is mellower. It might be available in large supermarkets and oriental food shops. It is peeled before use, then either sliced or chopped according to individual recipes. Sliced or chopped galangal can be kept in an airtight container in the refrigerator for up to 2 weeks; it also freezes well. Dried slices are also available: 1 dried slice is equivalent to $\frac{1}{2}$ inch of the fresh root. Powdered galangal can also be found, but it is not as good.

Garlic White garlic is a main ingredient in Thai cooking and is used in abundance. The size of the clove doesn't really affect the flavor, although very large cloves are milder.

Ginger Fresh ginger is readily available. Use it as galangal, above.

Glutinous rice This variety of short-grain rice is used in many Thai desserts. It is sometimes called "sticky" rice.

Krachai Also called lesser ginger, this root is smaller and fiercer than ginger and galangal, but should be treated in the same way. It may be available fresh or dried in oriental food shops.

Laver This type of seaweed can be found in many large supermarkets, health food stores, and oriental food shops.

Lemon grass Available from supermarkets, the straw-like tops and the ends of lemon grass should be trimmed, and the stalks thinly sliced. If you can't get fresh lemon grass, dried and powdered lemon grass are also available, or you can use lemon zest or juice as a substitute.

Limes and lime leaves The variety of lime grown in Thailand is called kaffir. It is slightly different from the limes we normally use, which make a perfectly adequate substitute. Kaffir lime leaves can be bought fresh or dried in oriental food shops and large supermarkets; if unavailable, use lime zest or juice, or lemon zest or juice as a last resort.

Mushrooms Many sorts of mushrooms are used in Thai cooking. These are a few:

Dried black fungus (cloud ear or wood ear mushrooms) can be found in oriental food shops. Soak them in warm water for 15–20 minutes, then drain before use.

Oyster mushrooms are available fresh from most supermarkets.

Shiitake mushrooms can be found dried in oriental food shops and some supermarkets, which might also sell them fresh. If dried, they should be soaked in warm water for about 15–20 minutes before use, then the hard stalk cut away and added to the stockpot.

Straw mushrooms can be found in cans in supermarkets.

Button, chestnut, and field mushrooms can be used if none of the others is available.

Noodles Many different kinds of noodles are used in Thai cooking, but the most commonly available are egg noodles, rice vermicelli, rice sticks, and glass noodles.

Egg noodles can be bought fresh from oriental shops, but the dried ones, which are widely available at supermarkets, are just as good.

Rice vermicelli are very thin and white, and become transparent when cooked. They are dried in long bundles, but can easily be cut into more convenient lengths with scissors.

Rice sticks are the same as vermicelli, only wider and flatter. They come in varying widths, and it is a matter of personal preference which ones you choose. Fresh rice sticks (Ho Fun) can be found in some oriental shops; these are white and slippery, and can be cut to any desired width. They do not keep well, and so should be used on the day of purchase.

Glass noodles are also known as cellophane noodles, bean-thread noodles, and bean vermicelli. They are very like rice vermicelli, but made from mung beans rather than rice.

Oil Groundnut oil is ideal, although corn oil or other vegetable oils can be used. Do not use olive oil, as the taste is too distinctive. After using oil for deep-frying, let it cool, then strain it through a fine sieve or cheesecloth back into the bottle for future use. If you like, you can then keep this oil specially for Thai cooking.

Oriental greens Thais use many different green vegetables in their cooking, including bok choy, choy sum, gai choy, Chinese cabbage and Chinese leaves. Many of these are available from supermarkets and specialist stores; use whichever you can get hold of.

Palm sugar This soft, raw, light brown sugar is widely used in Southeast Asia. In Thailand it is often sold wet, giving it a thick, honey-like consistency, but it is often exported in hard blocks that can be broken into pieces and dissolved. It tastes delicious and has a golden color that is especially attractive in desserts like coconut custard. If you can't get it, use a light muscovado or Indian jaggery suga, or light brown sugar as a last resort.

Paolo powder This special mixture of spices is available in Thai and oriental food stores.

Papaya Also called pawpaw, this tropical fruit is available from supermarkets. When unripe, the green flesh is used in salads. The orange flesh of ripe papaya tastes good with lime juice.

Red roast pork seasoning A special mixture of spices sold in Thai and oriental food stores.

Shrimp paste Available "fresh" or dried in plastic tubs or wrapped blocks, this is made of salted decomposed shrimp and is rich in Vitamin B. It is a major source of protein in many Southeast Asian diets. The dried blocks are stronger than the "fresh", but they are also very strong smelling. Available in oriental food shops.

Tamarind water Dried tamarind pulp can be found in oriental and Indian food shops. Simmer for 2–3 minutes in water, cool, then squeeze out the juice and discard the pulp and seeds. Tamarind concentrate can be bought in tubs—just dissolve a spoonful in hot water. You can substitute lemon juice.

Tofu Made from soy beans, tofu is highly nutritious and absorbs other flavors, making it a versatile addition to a vegetarian diet. There are several kinds of tofu available. One of the

Above: fresh flat egg noodles; Above right: fresh egg noodles; Far right: fresh ginger and krachai.

most useful types is fresh white tofu, which is sold in blocks in its own liquid. It is very delicate and will break up if stirred too much. Silken tofu is even more delicate. It does not keep long. Ready-cooked tofu is golden brown on the outside and much more solid. It is ideal for stir-frying. You can buy fairly solid white tofu cakes packed in water in plastic containers, which can be used for stir-frying if you can't get the ready-cooked kind. Sheets of tofu, sometimes called "bean-curd skins," are made from heated soy milk. They are dried, and need to be soaked for 2–3 hours before use. All of these products are available in health food stores, many supermarkets, and oriental food shops.

Turmeric This spice is a wonderful colorant with a very mild flavor. Although it can sometimes be found fresh in oriental and Asian food shops, it is most often used in its dried powder form.

Vinegar It is worth looking for white rice vinegar or distilled white vinegar in supermarkets or oriental food shops. If you cannot find it, use cider vinegar. Other vinegars will not suit oriental food.

Wonton wrappers Made from flour and eggs, these are deep yellow or brown in color. They are sold fresh or frozen in plastic bags, in oriental food shops. If a recipe uses differently shaped wrappers, cut them to shape with scissors. Otherwise, use sheets of phyllo pastry and cut them to the required shape.

Clockwise from left: panang curry paste; red curry paste; and green curry paste (pages 18–19)

basics

Many of the following basic recipes are for items that you can buy in ready-made versions. The majority of these are absolutely fine. However, it is interesting and useful to know how to make them yourself and, in the case of the exotic curry pastes, quite fun too. Of course you can buy all sorts of different Thai curry pastes these days: The best selections are found in oriental food stores. You can use stock cubes for your stock if you are in a rush, but don't forget to add some extra spices and herbs to cheer them up. Dried garlic and onion flakes work well if dry-fried.

Preparation time: 20 minutes

panang curry paste

- Put all the ingredients in a blender or food processor and blend to a smooth paste.
- Alternatively, you can pound all the ingredients together with a mortar and pestle.
- Transfer the paste to an airtight container and store in the refrigerator for up to 3 weeks.

4 shallots, chopped

8 garlic cloves, chopped

10 dried chiles, seeded

3 lemon grass stalks, chopped

3 cilantro roots

1-inch piece of fresh ginger, peeled and chopped

½ teaspoon coriander seeds, dry-fried

1 teaspoon cumin seeds, dry-fried

2 tablespoons Crushed Roasted Nuts (see page 24)

2 tablespoons groundnut oil

green curry paste

15 small fresh green chiles

4 garlic cloves, halved

2 lemon grass stalks, finely chopped

2 lime leaves, torn

2 shallots, chopped

1½ cups fresh cilantro leaves, stalks, and roots

1-inch piece of fresh ginger, chopped

2 teaspoons coriander seeds

1 teaspoon black peppercorns

1 teaspoon lime zest

½ teaspoon salt

2 tablespoons groundnut oil

- Put all the ingredients in a blender or food processor and blend to a thick paste.
- Alternatively, put the chiles in a mortar and crush with the pestle, then add the garlic and crush with the chiles, and so on with all the other ingredients, finally mixing in the oil with a spoon.
- Transfer the paste to an airtight container and store in the refrigerator for up to 3 weeks.

Preparation time: 15 minutes

Preparation time: 15 minutes

red curry paste

10 large fresh red chiles

2 teaspoons coriander seeds

2-inch piece of galangal, peeled and finely chopped

1 lemon grass stalk, finely chopped

4 garlic cloves, halved

1 shallot, roughly chopped

1 teaspoon lime juice

2 tablespoons groundnut oil

○ Put all the ingredients in a blender or food processor and blend to a thick paste.

○ Alternatively, you can pound all the ingredients together with a mortar and pestle.

○ Transfer the paste to an airtight container and store in the refrigerator for up to 3 weeks.

rice
kao

There are several methods of cooking rice. A great many Thais use electric rice steamers these days, but the following recipe has been used by people all over Southeast Asia for centuries. I recommend using Thai jasmine or fragrant rice. Although it is more expensive than other long-grain rice, it is superb quality, tastes delicious, and is what you would be eating were you in Thailand. I generally cook about 1 cup of rice per person, unless I am cooking several dishes, when I might cook only ½ cup per person.

1 lb Thai jasmine or
   fragrant rice
2 quarts water

○ Rinse the rice several times in a large bowl of water until the water is clear of rice starch. Drain thoroughly.
○ Bring the measured water to a boil in a saucepan and put the rice into it, giving it a stir to ensure that the grains are not stuck together in clumps. Bring back to a boil and cook, stirring occasionally, for 5–6 minutes.
○ Drain the rice into a metal colander and place it over another saucepan of boiling water, making sure that the level of the water is well beneath the rice. Take a chopstick and push it through the rice to the colander, to leave a steam hole. Do this in several places. Place a saucepan lid over the rice in the colander—it should not touch the rice—and steam for about 15 minutes, topping up the water level if necessary.
○ Remove the lid, fluff up the rice a little with a fork, and let it steam for about 3–4 minutes more. It will now be ready to serve. You can cook your rice in this way well in advance of your meal and just leave it covered until 10 minutes before you need it, then bring the water back to a boil and warm the rice again. You can also thaw frozen rice quite quickly using this method.

Preparation time: 5 minutes
Cooking time: 20–25 minutes

Preparation time: 1–2 minutes
Cooking time: 3–5 minutes

ground roast rice

2 tablepsoons uncooked rice

- Dry-fry the rice in a frying pan, using no oil. Shake and stir it around constantly until it turns a lovely golden color. Remove from the heat and allow to cool.
- Grind the rice using a mortar and pestle, or in a clean coffee or spice grinder.
- If you like, you can make a larger quantity, then store what you do not need immediately. Ground roast rice will keep up to 1 month in an airtight container in the refrigerator.

crispy basil

You can make Crispy Mint in the same way, using 2 cups fresh mint leaves.

2 tablespoons groundnut oil
1 cup fresh basil leaves
1 small fresh red chile, finely
  sliced

- Heat the oil in a wok until it is hot, add the basil and chile, and stir-fry for 1 minute until crispy. Remove with a slotted spoon and drain on paper towels.

Preparation time: 2 minutes
Cooking time: 1 minute

Preparation time: 5 minutes

garlic oil

6 tablespoons chopped garlic
1¼ cups groundnut oil
1 teaspoon ground black
  pepper

○ Put all the ingredients into an airtight container and leave to stand for 1 week before using.

crispy garlic and shallots

Thai people usually flavor their oil with garlic and shallots before using it. The crispy garlic and shallots are drained from the oil, reserved, and then sprinkled onto many different dishes. If you like, you can deep-fry just garlic or shallots, or you can deep-fry them both, as here, and store them together rather than separately. It's all a matter of personal choice.

about 3¼ cups groundnut oil,
  for deep-frying
3 tablespoons finely chopped
  garlic
¼ cup finely chopped shallots

○ Heat the oil for deep-frying in a wok. When the oil is good and hot, throw in the garlic and stir for about 40 seconds, watching it sizzle and turn golden.
○ Remove the garlic with a slotted spoon, draining as much oil as possible back into the wok, then spread the garlic out to dry on paper towels. Repeat the process with the shallots, allowing 1½–2 minutes frying time.
○ When the garlic and shallots are dried and crispy, you can store them in separate airtight containers, where they will keep for up to 1 month.
○ When the groundnut oil is cold, return it to an airtight container, to be reused.

Preparation time: 5 minutes
Cooking time: 2–2½ minutes

Preparation time: 1–2 minutes
Cooking time: 3–5 minutes

crushed roasted nuts

¼ cup unroasted peanuts or
cashew nuts

○ Dry-fry the nuts in a skillet, using no oil. Stir them around constantly until they turn a lovely golden color. Remove from the heat and allow to cool.

○ Place the nuts in a plastic bag and break into small pieces using a rolling pin.

○ You can roast and crush a larger quantity of nuts, then store what you do not need in an airtight container in the refrigerator for up to 1 month.

vegetable stock

2 large onions, quartered
4 large fresh red chiles
8 oz carrots, halved
¼ small white cabbage, halved
1 small head of celery
  (including leaves), chopped
1⅓ cups fresh cilantro leaves,
  stalks, and roots
1 cup fresh basil leaves
  and stalks
½ head Chinese leaves,
  chopped
½ mooli radish, peeled
25 black peppercorns
½ teaspoon salt
1 teaspoon palm sugar or light
  muscovado or brown sugar
8¾ cups water

○ Put all the ingredients, including the water, into a large, heavy-based saucepan. Bring to a boil, cover, and simmer for 1 hour.

○ Remove the lid and boil hard for 10 minutes. Allow to cool, then strain. Freeze any stock you are not using immediately.

Makes 7½ cups
Preparation time: 5–10 minutes
Cooking time: about 1 hour 30 minutes

Makes 2 litres/3½ pints
Preparation time: 3 minutes
Cooking time: 1 hour

fish stock

1 lb heads and bones of raw
   white fish, and heads and
   shells of shrimp, if available
2½ quarts water
3 shallots
1 celery stalk, including leaves,
   roughly chopped
1 lime leaf
½ stalk lemon grass
2 garlic cloves
¾ cup cilantro stalks
   and roots

- Put the fish heads and bones and water into a saucepan and bring to a boil. Skim off any foam that rises to the top.
- Add the shallots, celery, lime leaf, lemon grass, garlic and cilantro and simmer for 50 minutes.
- Strain the stock and freeze what you do not need to use immediately.

chicken stock

3½ lb boiling chicken
1 lb chicken giblets
1 onion, halved
1 carrot, roughly chopped
2 celery stalks, including leaves,
   roughly chopped
2 garlic cloves
1 stalk lemon grass, roughly
   chopped
10 black peppercorns
2 quarts water
1 lime leaf
3 large red chiles

- Put the chicken into a large heavy-based saucepan with the giblets, onion, carrot, and celery, and just cover them with the cold water. Place over a very low heat and bring to a boil as slowly as possible, about 50 minutes. When the water begins to simmer, remove the dark foam from the top until only white foam rises.
- Add the remaining ingredients and cook slowly for 2 hours, covered. Use a heat diffuser if you need to.
- Remove the chicken and set aside for another use. Strain the stock without pressing the juices from the vegetables—this helps to keep it clear. Use as much as you need and freeze what you do not need to use immediately.

Makes 6½ cups
Preparation time: 3 minutes
Cooking time: 2 hours 50 minutes

From left: crispy wrapped shrimp; stuffed chicken wings (pages 28–29)

snacks
and *appetizers*

Thai people don't have the conception of appetizers that Westerners do, but they certainly eat lots of snacks. All day long the little food stalls that line the streets do a roaring trade, each one specializing in a few chosen dishes. One or other of these dishes might well appear as part of a Thai meal, but can equally well be served separately as an appetizer if you prefer. Cook several of them for a light lunch or spear them with toothpicks and serve them as finger food at a party.

Preparation time: 10–15 minutes
Cooking time: 5 minutes

crispy wrapped shrimp

kung hom pa

⅓ cup ground pork
4 raw shrimp, shelled and
  minced
½ teaspoon sugar
¼ onion, finely chopped
1 garlic clove, finely chopped
2 teaspoons light soy sauce
12 raw shrimp
12 egg roll wrappers
beaten egg white, for sticking
about 3¼ cups oil,
  for deep-frying
Hot Sweet Sauce (see page
  114), to serve

To garnish:
sprig of basil or cilantro leaves
lime slices

○ Combine the ground pork, 4 minced raw shrimp, sugar, onion, garlic, and soy sauce in a bowl and set aside.

○ Shell the other 12 shrimp, leaving the tails intact, and carefully cut them open, making sure you do not cut right through them.

○ Put 1 teaspoon or more of the pork mixture onto each opened shrimp. Take an egg roll wrapper and pull one corner about three-quarters of the way toward the opposite corner. Place a shrimp onto the double thickness of wrapper, leaving the tail free, and roll it up, tucking in the ends and sticking down the wrapper with a little egg white. Continue until all shrimp are wrapped.

○ Heat the oil in a wok and deep-fry the shrimp rolls until golden, about 5 minutes. Remove from the wok and drain on paper towels.

○ Garnish with basil or cilantro leaves, slices of lime, and serve with a bowl of hot sweet sauce.

Preparation time: 35 minutes
Cooking time: 21 minutes

stuffed chicken wings

peagai yat sai

8 chicken wings

6 oz ground pork

2 teaspoons palm sugar or
  light muscovado or brown
  sugar

2½ tablespoons light soy sauce

pinch of black pepper

6 tablespoons finely chopped
  onion

¼ cup peas

2 oz rice vermicelli, soaked for
  15–20 minutes and cut into
  1-inch lengths

about 3¼ cups oil,
  for deep-frying

Hot Sweet Sauce (see page
  114), to serve

- Remove the main bones from the chicken wings by loosening the meat around the top with a knife and pulling it down over the bones.
- Place the ground pork, sugar, soy sauce, pepper, onion, peas, and rice vermicelli in a bowl and mix them thoroughly.
- Fill each wing with an equal amount of stuffing and pull the chicken meat shut at the end, enclosing all of the stuffing. The wings should now appear as they did before boning.
- Place the stuffed wings in a steamer and steam for 15 minutes.
- Heat the oil in a wok, transfer the wings from the steamer, and deep-fry them until they are golden, about 6 minutes.
- Serve the wings with hot sweet sauce.

Preparation time: 10–15 minutes, plus marinating
Cooking time: 10 minutes

chicken satay
satay gai

1 lb boneless, skinless chicken
breast, thinly sliced into
1 x 2-inch slices
bamboo skewers, soaked in
water for 30 minutes
Easy Satay Sauce (see page
117), to serve

Marinade:
1 tablespoon ground
cinnamon
1 tablespoon ground cumin
1 teaspoon ground black
pepper
⅔ cup oil
7 tablespoons light soy sauce
2 tablespoons palm sugar or
light muscovado or brown
sugar

To garnish:
raw onion, roughly chopped
cucumber chunks

○ Put the chicken slices into a large container and add all the ingredients for the marinade. Stir very thoroughly and make sure that all the chicken pieces are coated in the marinade. Leave for a minimum of 4 hours, but preferably overnight. Give it an occasional stir.

○ Carefully thread the chicken pieces onto the bamboo skewers, leaving some space at either end. Place the skewers under a hot broiler for about 2 minutes, turning once. As you cannot see if the chicken is cooked through, test one piece—you can always broil it for a little longer if necessary.

○ If you have to cook the skewers in batches, keep the cooked chicken warm while waiting for them all to be done.

○ Garnish with chopped raw onion and chunks of cucumber, and serve with easy satay sauce.

Preparation time: 12–14 minutes
Cooking time: 30 minutes

stuffed peppers
prik yat sai

4 bell peppers, red, green, or
  yellow
5 garlic cloves
8 cilantro roots
9 oz ground pork
1 tablespoon light soy sauce
½ teaspoon ground black
  pepper

To garnish:
Thai Egg Strips (see below)
cilantro leaves

- Carefully core and seed the peppers. Pound the garlic and cilantro roots together in a mortar until well broken down, about 2–3 minutes.
- Place the pork in a bowl and add the garlic and cilantro mixture, soy sauce, and pepper. Mix thoroughly and leave to stand for 7–8 minutes.
- Fill the peppers with the pork mixture, then place in a steamer and steam for about 30 minutes.
- Transfer the peppers to a dish and if liked, cut each one into 3–4 slices, arranging them so that they look whole.
- Serve garnished with egg strips and cilantro leaves.

thai egg strips
kai tiaow

3 eggs, beaten
1 shallot, finely sliced
green shoots of 1 scallion,
  sliced
1–2 small fresh red chiles,
  finely chopped
1 tablespoon chopped fresh
  cilantro leaves
1 tablespoon groundnut oil
salt and pepper
julienne of scallion,
  to garnish (optional)

- Mix all the ingredients, except the oil, in a bowl.
- Heat the oil in a skillet or wok, pour in the egg mixture, and swirl it around to produce a large thin omelet. Cook for 1–2 minutes until firm.
- Slide the omelet out onto a plate and roll it up. Allow to cool.
- When the omelet is cool, cut the roll crosswise into ¼-inch or ½-inch sections, depending on how wide you would like the strips to be. Serve them still rolled up or straightened out, in a heap. Garnish with strips of scallion, if wished.

Preparation time: 5 minutes
Cooking time: 2–3 minutes

Preparation time: 20 minutes
Cooking time: 15 minutes

son-in-law eggs
kai luk kuhy

4 hard-cooked eggs
about 3¼ cups groundnut oil,
  for deep-frying
5 shallots, finely sliced
3 large garlic cloves, finely
  sliced
5 tablespoons tamarind water
¼ cup fish sauce or
  1 teaspoon salt
¼ cup palm sugar or light
  muscovado or brown sugar
5 tablespoons water

To garnish:
2 large fresh red chiles, seeded
  and thinly sliced lengthwise
fresh cilantro leaves

- Peel the eggs and cut them in half lengthwise.
- Heat the oil for deep-frying in a wok and add the shallots and garlic. Cook gently until golden. Remove with a slotted spoon, drain on paper towels, and set aside.
- Slide the eggs, yolk side down, into the hot oil. Cook until golden all over, then remove with a slotted spoon. Drain and set aside.
- In a saucepan, put the tamarind water, fish sauce, and sugar. Stir until the sugar has melted, then add the water. Cook for 5 minutes, stirring all the time until the sauce becomes syrupy. Lower the heat.
- Arrange the eggs, yolk side up, on a plate. Sprinkle the shallots and garlic over them. Bring the sauce to a hard boil and continue boiling until the sauce is somewhat reduced and thickened. Remove from the heat and then ladle the sauce over the eggs.
- Serve hot, garnished with the red chile slivers and cilantro leaves.

shrimp and corn fritters
tod mun kung

2 tablespoons self-raising flour

⅓ cup raw shrimp, minced

1 teaspoon Red Curry Paste
(see page 19)

¼ cup corn kernels

1 egg white

1 lime leaf, shredded

oil, for deep-frying

cilantro sprigs, to garnish
(optional)

To serve:

Hot Sweet Sauce (see
page 114)

Soy and Vinegar Dipping Sauce
(see page 113)

- Mix the flour, minced shrimp, red curry paste, corn kernels, egg white, and lime leaf thoroughly in a bowl.
- Heat the oil in a wok over a moderate heat, then put 1 heaping tablespoon of the mixture at a time into the hot oil. You may want to do this in batches. Cook until golden brown, about 5 minutes.
- Remove the fritters from the wok and drain on paper towels, then arrange them on a serving dish.
- Garnish with sprigs of cilantro, if using, and serve with the dipping sauces.

Preparation time: 5 minutes
Cooking time: 10 minutes

shrimp and pork toast
kanoom bung nar gung

about 3¼ cups oil,
for deep-frying

⅓ cup ground pork

8 raw shrimps, minced

1 teaspoon sugar

¼ onion, finely chopped

2 large garlic cloves, finely
chopped

1 tablespoon light soy sauce

1 egg

4 slices white bread

2 teaspoons sesame seeds

basil sprigs, to garnish

- Heat the oil in a wok and, while it is heating, mix the pork, shrimps, sugar, onion, garlic, soy sauce, and egg thoroughly in a bowl. Spread the mixture on the slices of bread and press sesame seeds onto it.
- Slide the bread into the wok, spread side up, 2 pieces at a time, and deep-fry over a moderate heat for about 5 minutes, or until golden. Turn each slice over and cook for 30 seconds, then remove from the oil and drain on paper towels.
- Cut each slice into 4 pieces, arrange on a serving dish, and garnish with a few sprigs of basil.
- Serve with the dipping sauces in individual bowls.

Preparation time: 10 minutes
Cooking time: 11 minutes

To serve:

Hot Sweet Sauce (see
page 114)

Soy and Vinegar Dipping Sauce
(see page 113)

egg rolls *bapia tod*

12 square egg roll wrappers
about 3¼ cups groundnut oil,
   for deep-frying
12 toothpicks
cilantro leaves, to garnish
Lime and Fish Sauce and Hot
   Sweet Sauce (see page 114),
   to serve

Filling:

1 tablespoon groundnut oil
2 garlic cloves, finely chopped
⅔ cup beansprouts
½ cup shredded white cabbage
2 fresh shiitake mushrooms,
   shredded
2½ tablespoons finely chopped
   celery (leaf and stalk)
1 teaspoon sugar
2 teaspoons soy sauce
2 oz dried glass noodles,
   soaked, drained, and cut into
   short lengths with scissors

○ First make the filling: heat the wok and add the oil, garlic, beansprouts, cabbage, mushrooms and celery. Stir-fry for 30 seconds, then add the sugar, soy sauce, and noodles. Stir-fry for 1 minute, then remove from the heat and place the mixture on a plate. Wipe the wok clean with paper towels.

○ Put 1 tablespoon of the filling on one corner of an egg roll wrapper, then roll it up, wrapping in the ends to form a neat tube. Use a little oil to stick down the last corner, then secure the roll with a toothpick. Repeat with the remaining wrappers and filling.

○ Heat the oil for deep-frying in a wok, pop in a batch of egg rolls, and cook over a moderate heat for 3–4 minutes until golden brown on all sides. Remove from the oil with a slotted spoon and drain on paper towels. Repeat with the remaining egg rolls.

○ Remove the toothpicks before serving and serve hot, garnished with cilantro leaves, and with the dipping sauces in individual bowls.

Preparation time: 15–20 minutes, plus soaking
Cooking time: 12 minutes

Preparation time: 15–20 minutes, plus soaking
Cooking time: 12 minutes

shrimp egg rolls
bapia tod gung

12 square egg roll wrappers
about 3¼ cups oil,
  for deep-frying
12 toothpicks

Filling:
2 tablespoons oil
5 oz raw shrimp, shelled and
  finely chopped
2 oz rice vermicelli, soaked for
  15–20 minutes, drained, and
  cut into short lengths
2½ tablespoons grated carrot
⅓ cup shredded white cabbage
¼ cup beansprouts
2 tablespoons light soy sauce
1 tablespoon sugar

To serve:
lettuce leaves
sliced tomatoes
Hot Sweet Sauce
  (see page 114)

- First make the filling: Heat the oil in a wok, add the shrimp, vermicelli, carrot, cabbage, and beansprouts, and stir-fry for 1 minute. Add the soy sauce and sugar, stir-fry for 2 minutes, then remove from the heat and put the ingredients on a plate to cool. Wipe the wok clean with paper towels.

- Put 1 tablespoon of the filling onto one corner of an egg roll wrapper and roll it up, tucking in the ends to form a neat tube. Use a little oil or egg white to stick down the last corner, then secure the roll with a toothpick.

- Heat the oil for deep-frying in the wok and pop in a batch of egg rolls. Cook them for 3–4 minutes until they are golden brown on all sides. Remove with a slotted spoon and drain on paper towels. Repeat with the remaining egg rolls.

- Remove the toothpicks before serving. Place the egg rolls on a bed of lettuce leaves and sliced tomatoes, and serve with the hot sweet sauce in a separate bowl.

Preparation time: 15 minutes
Cooking time: 30 minutes

steamed wonton
kanom jeeb

16 wonton wrappers
a little oil

Filling:
6 raw shrimp, shelled
½ cup ground pork
6 tablespoons chopped onion
2 garlic cloves
5 water chestnuts
1 teaspoon palm sugar or light
   muscovado or brown sugar
1 tablespoon light soy sauce
1 egg

To serve:
Soy and Vinegar Dipping Sauce
   (see page 113)
Hot Sweet Sauce
   (see page 114)

○ First make the filling: blend all the ingredients in a blender or food processor.

○ Form a circle with the index finger and thumb of one hand, and place a wonton wrapper on top. Put 1 heaping teaspoonful of the filling into the center of the wrapper. As you push the filled wrapper down through the circle of your fingers, tighten the top, shaping it but leaving it open. Repeat this process with all of the wrappers.

○ Put the filled wontons onto a plate and place the plate in a steamer. Drizzle a little oil on top of the wontons, cover, and steam for 30 minutes.

○ Serve the wontons hot or warm, with the dipping sauces served separately.

From left: pork ball and black fungus soup; chicken and coconut milk soup (pages 42–43)

soups

Soup is usually part of a Thai meal—even breakfast, which is often a rice soup. Noodle soups are eaten throughout Southeast Asia as light meals in themselves. Cooked noodles—they can be made of rice, bean or egg, and may be wide or narrow, dried or fresh— are placed in the bowl first and then the bowl is filled with steaming stock. Next come pieces of chicken or pork, shrimp, meat or fish balls, and the whole lot is garnished with cilantro leaves, crispy shallots or garlic, sliced scallions, and chiles. Lighter soups form part of a meal. Thais don't drink with their meals as a rule and a few spoonfuls of soup now and then probably help the rest of the meal go down!

Preparation time: 10 minutes
Cooking time: 10 minutes

chicken and coconut milk soup
tom ka gai

This quantity of soup is enough for 1 large bowl of soup shared between 4 people or for 4 small, individual bowls. If you would like to serve the soup as a first course on its own, just double the quantities.

1¼ cups Chicken Stock (see
   page 25)

3 lime leaves, torn

½ stalk lemon grass,
   obliquely sliced

1-inch piece galangal, peeled
   and finely sliced

7 tablespoons coconut milk

¼ cup fish sauce

1 teaspoon palm sugar or light
   muscovado or brown sugar

3 tablespoons lime juice

½ cup bite-sized pieces skinless
   chicken

2 tablespoons chile oil or
   2 small chiles, finely sliced
   (optional)

○ Heat the stock and add the lime leaves, lemon grass, and galangal. Stir them in and, as the stock is simmering, add the coconut milk, fish sauce, sugar, and lime juice. Give it a good stir, then add the chicken pieces and simmer for 5 minutes.

○ Just before serving, add the chile oil or chiles, if you like, stir again, and serve.

Preparation time: 5 minutes, plus soaking
Cooking time: 10 minutes

pork ball and black fungus soup

tom jieu won sen

This soup is usually served with Shrimp Paste Rice with Chicken (see page 105).

2½ cups Chicken Stock (see
  page 25)
2 garlic cloves, sliced
½ cup ground pork
3 dried black fungi, soaked for
  30 minutes and sliced
2 tablespoons light soy sauce
1 tablespoon fish sauce
2 oz rice vermicelli, soaked for
  15–20 minutes and cut into
  2-inch lengths

- Heat the stock and add the garlic.
- Shape the pork into little round balls. Drop them into the stock and simmer for 5 minutes.
- Add the black fungus, soy sauce, fish sauce, and rice vermicelli. Cook for about 2 minutes and serve.

red pork noodle soup *ba mie mu daeng*

- Put the egg noodles into plenty of water and boil for 2–3 minutes, untangling them while they are boiling. Drain, and mix in the garlic oil to prevent sticking.
- Boil the choi sum for 1 minute, drain, and reserve.
- Place the noodles in a large serving bowl, then add the choi sum, scallion, soy sauce, cilantro leaves, and black pepper. Arrange the pork slices on the top. Heat the chicken stock to boiling point and pour it over the pork, noodles, and vegetables.
- Combine all the ingredients for the dipping sauce in a small bowl and serve with the soup.

Preparation time: 10 minutes
Cooking time: 5 minutes

6 oz fresh egg noodles
1 teaspoon Garlic Oil (see page 22)
2 choi sum, sliced
1 tablespoon finely sliced scallion
1 tablespoon light soy sauce
¼ cup cilantro leaves
pinch of black pepper
⅓ recipe Red Roast Pork, sliced (see page 58)
2½ cups Chicken Stock (see page 25)

Dipping sauce:
¼ cup distilled white vinegar
2–3 tablespoons fish sauce
1 large red chile, sliced

pork and bamboo shoot soup *tom jieu moo sup nomai*

- Heat the stock, then add the peppercorns and crushed and chopped garlic.
- Meanwhile, mix the pork with the pepper and soy sauce, and form into small meat balls. Put them into the simmering stock and cook for 4 minutes. Add the bamboo shoots and simmer gently for 5 minutes. Add the fish sauce, give the soup a good stir, and serve garnished with the scallion and cilantro leaves.

Preparation time: 6–8 minutes
Cooking time: 15 minutes

1 pint Chicken Stock (see page 25)
10 black peppercorns, crushed
2 garlic cloves, crushed
5 garlic cloves, roughly chopped
½ cup ground pork
pinch of black pepper
1½ tablespoons light soy sauce
¾ cup bamboo shoots
3 tablespoons fish sauce

To garnish:
1 scallion, obliquely sliced
cilantro leaves

Preparation time: 10 minutes
Cooking time: 12 minutes

noodle soup with chicken

kwetio nam gai

This soup is sufficient on its own for a light meal for 4 people. If you wish to serve it as part of a Thai meal, you should halve or even quarter the quantities.

○ Put the stock, star anise, cinnamon, pickled garlic, vinegar, fish sauce, cilantro roots, sugar, and soy sauce into a large saucepan and bring slowly to a boil.

○ Add the chicken and simmer for 4 minutes.

○ Add the green vegetables and beansprouts, and simmer for 2 minutes.

○ To serve, divide the rice sticks between 4 large soup bowls and ladle the soup over them. Sprinkle the cilantro leaves on top and garnish with crispy shallots.

5 cups Chicken Stock (see page 25)
1 star anise
3-inch piece of cinnamon stick, broken up
2 bulbs Pickled Garlic (see page 110), finely chopped
¼ cup pickled garlic vinegar
½ cup fish sauce
8 cilantro roots, finely chopped
4 teaspoons palm sugar or light muscovado or brown sugar
4 teaspoons light soy sauce
1 cup diced skinless chicken
1⅓ cups roughly chopped green vegetables, such as spring cabbage, chard, or pak choi
⅔ cup beansprouts
7 oz rice sticks, cooked
½ cup cilantro leaves
Crispy Shallots (see page 22), to garnish

pork ball and tofu soup *tom jieu loo chin tahu*

2½ cups Chicken Stock (see
  page 25) or stock remaining
  from cooking Chicken with
  Rice (see page 71)
1 garlic clove, finely chopped
4 garlic cloves, halved
½ teaspoon ground black
  pepper
8 cilantro roots
1 cup silken tofu, cut into
  1-inch slices
1 sheet roasted laver, torn
  into shreds
2 tablespoons light soy sauce
cilantro leaves, to garnish

Pork balls:
⅓ cup ground pork
1 tablespoon light soy sauce
½ teaspoon ground black
  pepper

- Heat the stock, in a saucepan with the chopped and halved garlic, pepper, and cilantro roots.
- While the soup is heating, make the pork balls. Combine the pork, soy sauce, and pepper, form the mixture into small balls, drop them into the soup, and simmer gently for 6–7 minutes.
- Add the tofu, laver, and soy sauce, stir for 30 seconds, then serve garnished with the cilantro leaves.

Preparation time: 3–4 minutes
Cooking time: 12–13 minutes

mussel soup
tom jieu hoi

1 lb mussels
1¼ cups coconut milk
2½ cups Fish Stock (see page 25)
3 oz rice vermicelli, soaked for 15–20 minutes
1 tablespoon finely chopped ginger
1 cup cilantro stems and roots
½ stalk lemon grass, chopped
2 small red chiles, finely sliced
1 tablespoon fish sauce
1 tablespoon lime juice
1 cup cilantro leaves, to garnish

- Clean the mussels thoroughly, remove the beards, and leave in a bowl of cold water for about 1 hour. Drain and tap any open shells to ensure they close. Discard any that remain open.
- Put the mussels into a saucepan, cover, and cook over a moderate heat for about 3–4 minutes. The mussels will open and release their liquid. Any that remain closed should be thrown away. Remove the mussels with a slotted spoon and reserve.
- Add the remaining ingredients and simmer for 15 minutes.
- Return the mussels to the pot and simmer for 1 minute. Serve, garnished with cilantro leaves.

hot and sour shrimp soup
tom yam kung

5 cups Fish Stock (see page 25)
4 lime leaves, torn
1 stalk lemon grass, finely and obliquely sliced
1-inch piece galangal, sliced
1 tablespoon palm sugar or light muscovado sugar
5 tablespoons lime juice
2 tablespoons chile oil or 12 small green chiles, chopped
12–16 raw shrimp
salt and pepper
cilantro sprigs, to garnish

- Place the stock, lime leaves, lemon grass, galangal, sugar, lime juice, and chile oil or chopped chiles in a large wok or saucepan and bring to a boil. Lower the heat and allow the soup to simmer gently for 15 minutes.
- Add the shrimp just before serving; they will turn pink in a few seconds and will be cooked through after 1 minute.
- Check the seasoning and serve the soup in 1 large bowl or 4 individual bowls. Garnish with sprigs of cilantro.

Preparation time: 5 minutes
Cooking time: 20 minutes

From left: beef curry country style; chile pork (pages 52–53)

pork
and *beef*

Meat is really still food for a special occasion throughout most of Thailand. Beef is much less common than pork; there are few cattle in the country and a lot of the indigenous "beef" is actually buffalo. The diet is all the healthier for the small quantities of meat, although every now and then, for a feast day or a celebration of some kind, a lot of meat is served, although you probably wouldn't be able to recognize most of it! Pork appears in numerous forms and in very different styles. For example, there is a spicy pork sausage that is common to northern Thailand but is not found in many other parts of the country, except, of course, Bangkok, to which people from all over Thailand migrate in search of a better life, bringing their local delicacies with them.

Preparation time: 10 minutes
Cooking time: 6–8 minutes

chile pork
nam prik ong

5 small shallots

10–15 small dried chiles,
  soaked for 20 minutes

12 cilantro roots

3 tablespoons oil

½ cup ground pork

2 tomatoes, diced

5 teaspoons sugar

5 teaspoons fish sauce

cilantro leaves, to garnish

Salad:

½ cucumber, cut into chunks

1 baby romaine or little gem
  lettuce, separated into leaves

cilantro sprigs

- Put the shallots, chiles, and cilantro roots into a food processor or blender and blend, adding a little water if the mixture seems very dry. Alternatively, pound them together in a mortar for 5–8 minutes until thoroughly amalgamated.
- Heat the oil in a wok, add the chile paste, and stir-fry for 30 seconds. Add the pork and tomatoes, and cook, stirring, for 30 seconds. Add the sugar and fish sauce, and continue to cook, stirring, for 4–5 minutes.
- Transfer the pork to a bowl, garnish with cilantro, and serve, with the salad arranged on a separate plate.

Preparation time: 8 minutes
Cooking time: about 20 minutes

beef curry country style
gang bar nua

1 tablespoon oil

2 tablespoons Red Curry
Paste (see page 19)

½ cup thin, bite-sized pieces
lean rump steak

3-inch piece krachai, washed
and cut into julienne strips

1¼ cups Chicken Stock
(see page 25)

3 tablespoons fish sauce

3 tablespoons palm sugar or
light muscovado sugar

12 ears baby corn,
obliquely sliced

3 oz sugar snap peas

⅔ cup bamboo shoots

1–2 large red chiles, obliquely
sliced

¼ cup chopped basil leaves

○ Heat the oil in a wok. Add the curry paste, beef, and krachai, and cook, stirring well, for 30 seconds. Add the stock and cook over a moderate heat for 2–3 minutes, stirring all the time, then add the fish sauce and sugar. Reduce the heat to low and cook for 10 more minutes.

○ Turn the heat to high and add all the vegetables and the chile, stirring well and turning for about 3 minutes. Add a little more stock if necessary.

○ To serve, stir in the basil and transfer the curry to a serving bowl.

Preparation time: 20 minutes
Cooking time: 9 minutes

pork with salted eggs and beansprouts

pad tua nok kai kem moo

2 Salted Eggs (see page 112),
  shelled and halved
2 tablespoons oil
1 garlic clove, chopped
⅓ cup ground pork
1 tablespoon oyster sauce
1 teaspoon sugar
¼ cup Chicken Stock (see
  page 25)
1 tablespoon fish sauce
2⅓ cups beansprouts
2 large red chiles, obliquely
  sliced
1 scallion, obliquely sliced
cilantro leaves, to garnish

- Allow the hard-cooked salted eggs to cool. Heat the oil in a wok and cook the garlic and pork for 3 minutes. Add the oyster sauce, sugar, stock, and fish sauce, and stir-fry for 5 minutes.
- Add the salted eggs and the remaining ingredients, and cook very briefly—about 1 minute—then transfer to a serving dish.
- Serve garnished with cilantro leaves.

pork with lime
moo manao

10 oz loin of pork, cut into
½ × 1-inch strips

2 tablespoons light soy sauce

½ teaspoon ground black
pepper

1 tablespoon oil

10 garlic cloves, chopped

15 small green chiles, chopped

¼ cup lime juice

¼ cup fish sauce

1 tablespoon palm sugar or
light muscovado sugar

⅔ cup finely chopped mint
leaves

In Thailand, the garlic in this dish is not cooked. However, you can fry it with the pork, if you prefer.

- Mix the pork, soy sauce, and pepper in a bowl.
- Heat the oil in a wok and add the pork mixture. Stir-fry over a high heat until the pork is well cooked, about 6 minutes.
- Transfer the pork to a mixing bowl or saucepan and add all of the remaining ingredients. Mix thoroughly for 1–2 minutes, then transfer to a serving dish.

Preparation time: 10–12 minutes
Cooking time: 6 minutes

steamed egg with ground pork
kai toon moo sup

½ cup ground pork

3 eggs

⅔ cup water

1 tablespoon oil

1½ tablespoons fish sauce

3 tablespoons chopped
cilantro leaves

2 tablespoons obliquely sliced
scallion

black pepper

Crispy Garlic and Shallots (see
page 22), to garnish

- Put the pork into a mixing bowl and break it up with a fork. Beat the eggs and combine well with the pork. Add the water, oil, and fish sauce, season well with pepper, and mix thoroughly.
- Transfer the pork mixture to a heat-proof bowl, sprinkle the cilantro and scallion on top, and steam, covered, for 40 minutes.
- To serve, sprinkle crispy garlic and shallots over the cilantro and scallion.

Preparation time: 5 minutes
Cooking time: 40 minutes

Preparation time: 10 minutes
Cooking time: 7 minutes

pork-stuffed omelet
kai yat sai moo

1 tablespoon oil
5 eggs, beaten
cilantro sprigs, to garnish

Filling:
¼ cup finely chopped onion
1 small red chile, finely sliced
½-inch lemon grass, finely sliced
2 tablespoons oil
¼ cup ground pork
1½ tomatoes, diced
2 tablespoons finely chopped
   mixed green, red, and yellow
   bell peppers
1 tablespoon corn kernels
1 tablespoon peas
5 tablespoons Easy Sweet and
   Sour Sauce (see page 116)

- First make the filling: pound the onion, chile, and lemon grass in a mortar until well broken down, then set aside.
- Heat the oil in a wok, add the onion mixture, and stir-fry for 30 seconds. Add all the remaining ingredients and stir-fry over a high heat for 2 minutes.
- Remove the filling from the wok and set aside.
- Wipe the wok clean with paper towels.
- To make the omelet, put the 1 tablespoon of oil into the wok and heat it, making sure that the oil coats not only the base of the wok but as much of the sides as possible. Pour in the eggs, swirling them around to make a large thin omelet.
- When the omelet is almost firm, add the filling and fold the edges over to form a square parcel. Make sure the parcel does not stick to the bottom of the pan.
- Carefully slide the omelet onto a serving plate, garnish with sprigs of cilantro, and serve at once.

Preparation time: 5 minutes, plus marinating
Cooking time: 1–1¼ hours
Oven temperature: 400°F

red roast pork
mu daeng

1½ lb pork shoulder, spare rib, or leg, boned and rolled, with fat removed

1 packet (2 oz) red roast pork seasoning mix

1 tablespoon tomato paste

2 tablespoons palm sugar or light muscovado sugar

1 tablespoon Chicken Stock (see page 25)

To garnish:
cilantro leaves
fresh chiles

I think it is worth making a large quantity of this, as it can be used in many other dishes (see page 44) and is delicious cold as well as hot. However, if you prefer, you can simply halve the quantities in the recipe and you will have sufficient for 4 people as part of a Thai meal.

- Cut the pork into 4 large chunks, put them into a bowl, and mix in all the other ingredients thoroughly, making sure that all the pork is coated. Cover and leave to marinate for a minimum of 5 hours, preferably overnight.
- Preheat the oven to 400°F. Place the pork in a roasting pan and cook for 1–1¼ hours, turning occasionally.
- To serve, slice the pork thinly, arrange on a serving dish, and garnish with cilantro leaves and chiles.

pork with bamboo shoots
moo nomai

2 tablespoons oil

1 tablespoon Red Curry Paste (see page 19)

⅔ cup Chicken Stock (see page 25)

½ cup bite-sized pieces of pork

1 tablespoon palm sugar or light muscovado sugar

2 tablespoons fish sauce

½ cup bamboo shoots

2 lime leaves, torn

- Heat the oil in a wok, add the red curry paste, and cook for 30 seconds.
- Add the stock, pork, sugar, and fish sauce, and cook, stirring, for 4–5 minutes. Increase the heat, add the bamboo shoots, and continue to cook for 1–2 minutes, then add the lime leaves.
- Give the pork a final stir, transfer to a bowl, and serve at once.

Preparation time: 4 minutes
Cooking time: 9–10 minutes

Preparation time: 2–3 minutes, plus marinating
Cooking time: 40 minutes
Oven temperature: 350°F

spare ribs
gat doog moo

4 large or 8 small pork spare
ribs, weighing about
I lb in total

Marinade:

I½ tablespoons palm sugar or
light muscovado sugar

3 tablespoons light soy sauce

I tablespoon oyster sauce

I teaspoon ground black
pepper

6 large garlic cloves, chopped

○ Combine all the marinade ingredients in a bowl. Add the spare ribs, turning them
thoroughly to coat them all over with the marinade. They need to marinate for a
minimum of 2 hours, but the longer you leave them, the tastier they will be.

○ Preheat the oven to 350°F. Place the spare ribs on a baking sheet, with as much of
the marinade as possible, and bake for 40 minutes.

sweet and sour
pork *peao wun moo*

2 tablespoons oil

½ cup thin slices of pork

¾ onion, sliced

I tomato, quartered

¼ cucumber, cut into chunks

⅓ cup fresh pineapple chunks

¼ cup thinly sliced green or red
bell pepper

7 tablespoons Easy Sweet and
Sour Sauce (see page 116)

○ Heat the oil in a wok. Add the pork and onion, and stir-fry over a high heat for
about 2 minutes.

○ Add the tomato, cucumber, pineapple, and green or red pepper, and stir-fry for
another 3 minutes.

○ Add the sweet and sour sauce, mix well, stirring constantly for 1 minute, and
serve at once.

Preparation time: 10 minutes
Cooking time: 6 minutes

Preparation time: 5 minutes
Cooking time: 14 minutes

panang beef curry
gang panang nua

1 tablespoon oil

1½ tablespoons Panang Curry Paste (see page 18)

6 tablespoons coconut milk

3 lime leaves, finely shredded

½ cup bite-sized pieces top round of beef

3 tablespoons Chicken Stock (see page 25)

1 large red chile, obliquely sliced

3 tablespoons palm sugar or light muscovado sugar

½ cup peas

2 lime leaves, torn, to garnish

○ Heat the oil in a wok, add the curry paste, and cook for 30 seconds.

○ Pour in the coconut milk, add the lime leaves, and stir and cook for 1 minute.

○ Add the beef, stock, chile, and sugar, and increase the heat. Cook, stirring, for 1 minute, then reduce the heat and simmer for 7 minutes.

○ Add the peas to the wok and simmer for 3 more minutes. The sauce should thicken considerably, but add a little more stock if you feel it is getting too dry.

○ Transfer the curry to a serving bowl and serve garnished with lime leaves.

stir-fried beef with oyster sauce
nua pad nam mon hoi

2 tablespoons oil

½ cup thinly sliced, bite-sized pieces rump steak

1 garlic clove, chopped

6 tablespoons sliced onion

¼ cup thinly sliced mixed green, red, and yellow bell peppers

1 cup fresh shiitake mushrooms

1½ tablespoons oyster sauce

¼ cup Chicken Stock (see page 25)

1 large red chile, obliquely sliced

1 teaspoon palm sugar or light muscovado sugar

2 tablespoons obliquely sliced scallion

pinch of black pepper

○ Heat the oil in a wok, add the beef, garlic, onion, mixed peppers, and mushrooms, and stir-fry over a fairly high heat for 2 minutes.

○ Add the oyster sauce, stock, chile, and sugar, and stir-fry for 2 minutes, then add the scallion and season with pepper.

○ Transfer to a serving platter, and serve.

Preparation time: 8–10 minutes
Cooking time: 5 minutes

Preparation time: 2 minutes
Cooking time: 6 minutes (for medium rare)

broiled beef with spicy sauce

neua yang nam tok

10 oz sirloin steak

Spicy sauce:
½ tomato, finely chopped
¼ red onion, finely chopped
1 tablespoon dried ground
  chile
6 tablespoons fish sauce
2 tablespoons lime juice or
  tamarind water
2 teaspoons palm sugar or
  light muscovado sugar
1 teaspoon Ground Roast Rice
  (see page 21)
1 tablespoon Chicken Stock
  (see page 25)

To garnish:
basil leaves
cilantro leaves
flat-leaf parsley
mixed chiles

- Put the steak under a preheated hot broiler and cook, turning it once, according to your taste.
- While it is cooking, combine all the sauce ingredients in a bowl.
- When the steak is ready, slice it and arrange on a serving dish. Garnish with the basil, cilantro leaves, parsley, and chiles. Serve the spicy sauce separately.

Chickens and ducks in Thailand do not have much in common with those we usually eat here—they are smaller, thinner, and tougher. However, unlike our tender but often rather bland-tasting birds, these taste superb. They spend their lives roaming around freely, feeding on whatever they find. Ducks splash about the paddy fields happily. Chicken and duck are often chopped before cooking. I suggest asking your butcher to do this for you—unless you are quite skilled you will find the bones splinter when you do it yourself. Thais do not generally skin their chicken, but I think that is a matter of personal preference. It is worth removing as much fat as you can, as all the recipes contain some oil or coconut milk.

chicken and *duck*

Preparation time: 15 minutes
Cooking time: 13–15 minutes

green curry chicken

gang keyo wun gai

1 tablespoon oil

1½ tablespoons Green Curry Paste (see page 18)

¼ cup coconut milk

½ cup bite-sized pieces chicken breast

2 lime leaves, torn

½ stalk lemon grass, cut in fine, oblique slices

⅓ cup bamboo shoots

3 small round green eggplants, cut into quarters

½ cup oblique chunks zucchini

1 large red chile, obliquely sliced

6 tablespoons Chicken Stock (see page 25)

1 tablespoon palm sugar or light muscovado or brown sugar

3 tablespoons fish sauce

sweet basil sprigs, to garnish

○ Heat the oil in a wok and stir in the curry paste. Cook for 30 seconds, then add the coconut milk, and cook, stirring, for 1 minute.

○ Add the chicken, bring up to a simmer, and add all the remaining ingredients. Simmer for 10 minutes, stirring occasionally.

○ Transfer the curry to a serving bowl, garnish with basil sprigs, and serve.

Preparation time: 15 minutes
Cooking time: 6 minutes

chile-fried duck
pad pet prik

¼ roast duck

2 tablespoons oil

3 large garlic cloves,
  finely chopped

½ onion, sliced

¼ cup sliced carrot

½ cup sliced mixed green, red,
  and yellow bell peppers

3 ears baby corn, obliquely
  sliced

1 broccoli floret, chopped

4 sugar snap peas or
  snow peas

2 small green chiles, finely
  sliced

1 teaspoon palm sugar or light
  muscovado or brown sugar

2 tablespoons light soy sauce

3 tablespoons Chicken Stock
  (see page 25)

basil leaves, to garnish

○ Take the skin and meat off the duck, chop into bite-sized pieces, and set aside.

○ Heat the oil in a wok, add the garlic, and stir-fry for 10 seconds. Add the duck, stir briefly, and then add the onion, carrot, mixed peppers, baby corn, broccoli, and sugar snap peas or snow peas. Stir-fry vigorously for 20 seconds, add the chile, and cook, stirring, for 45 seconds.

○ Finally, add the sugar, soy sauce, and chicken stock, mixing them thoroughly with the contents of the wok for 3 minutes.

○ Tranfer to a serving dish and garnish with basil leaves.

Preparation time: 10 minutes
Cooking time: 6 minutes

ground chicken with basil

pad grapao gai

5 small green chiles

2 garlic cloves

2 tablespoons oil

½ cup ground chicken

1 shallot, chopped

2 tablespoons bamboo shoots

¼ cup chopped red bell
    pepper

2 tablespoons diced carrot

1 teaspoon palm sugar or light
    muscovado or brown sugar

3 tablespoons fish sauce

3 tablespoons Chicken Stock
    (see page 25)

¼ cup finely chopped basil
    leaves

To garnish:
Crispy Garlic (see page 22)
Crispy Shallots (see page 22)
Crispy Basil (see page 21)

You can make ground chicken either by using a meat grinder or simply by putting the chicken in a food processor and pulsing it to the desired texture.

- Put the chiles and garlic into a mortar and pound together with a pestle until well broken down.
- Heat the oil in a wok, add the chiles and garlic, and stir-fry for 30 seconds. Add the remaining ingredients and cook over a medium heat, stirring, for 4 minutes. Turn the heat up high and continue stirring vigorously for 30 seconds.
- Transfer to a dish and serve with rice, garnished with the crispy garlic, crispy shallots, and crispy basil.

Preparation time: 10 minutes
Cooking time: 12–14 minutes

stir-fried chicken with pineapple
gai pad sapparote

about 3¼ cups oil,
  for deep-frying
½ cup tempura flour or
  self-raising flour
5 tablespoons water
½ cup bite-sized pieces
  skinless chicken
1 tablespoon oil
1 cup fresh pineapple chunks
1 tomato, cut into 8 pieces
1 tablespoon tomato paste
1 tablespoon palm sugar or
  light muscovado sugar
½ cup cashew nuts
1½ tablespoons light soy sauce

To garnish:
1 scallion, obliquely sliced
cilantro sprigs

- Heat the oil in a wok. While it is heating, mix the flour and water together thoroughly to make a batter.
- When the oil is hot enough, coat half the chicken pieces in the batter and deep-fry them until they are golden brown. Remove from the oil and drain them on paper towels. Repeat the process with the rest of the chicken.
- Pour off the oil, wipe the wok clean with paper towels, then heat 1 tablespoon of oil in it. Add the pineapple, tomato, tomato paste, sugar, and cashews, and stir-fry for 2 minutes.
- Add the soy sauce and stir. Return the batter-coated chicken to the wok and stir again over a high heat, then serve garnished with scallion and cilantro sprigs.

stir-fried chicken with ginger
gai pad king

2 tablespoons oil

¼ onion, chopped

2 garlic cloves, chopped

½ cup bite-sized pieces skinless chicken

3-inch piece fresh ginger, julienned

3 fresh shiitake mushrooms, sliced

1 tablespoon oyster sauce

1 tablespoon yellow beans

1 teaspoon palm sugar or light muscovado or brown sugar

3 tablespoons Chicken Stock (see page 25)

1 scallion, obliquely sliced, to garnish

- Heat the oil in a wok, add the onion, garlic, and chicken, and stir-fry for about 2 minutes. Add the ginger and mushrooms, and continue to stir-fry over a gentle heat for 2½ minutes. Add the oyster sauce, yellow beans, sugar, and stock, turn up the heat, and stir-fry for 30 seconds.
- Transfer to a serving dish, sprinkle with scallions, and serve.

Preparation time: 8 minutes
Cooking time: 5 minutes

chicken with rice
kao man gai

3 lb chicken

1 sprig cilantro leaves, stalk, and root

1 large garlic clove, chopped

2¾ cups rice, washed

cilantro leaves, to garnish

Sauce:

4 garlic cloves

4½-inch piece fresh ginger, julienned

1 heaping tablespoon yellow beans in salted sauce

4 large red chiles, halved

¼ cup cilantro stalk and root

2 tablespoons Chicken Stock (see page 25)

3 tablespoons lime juice

3 tablespoons light soy sauce

1 tablespoon sugar

- Skin the chicken and remove as much fat as you can. Place the chicken and skin in a casserole with enough water to cover, then add the cilantro sprig and garlic. Boil, covered, until cooked, about 1 hour. Reduce the heat to a minimum.
- Put the rice into a heavy-based saucepan and ladle over enough stock from the chicken pot to cover it. The liquid should be ¼ inch above the level of the rice. Bring the rice to a boil over a moderate heat, stir to make sure it does not stick together in lumps, and simmer, uncovered, until the rice has absorbed all the stock. Then lower the heat as much as you can, cover tightly, and leave to stand for 10–12 minutes.
- Take the rice off the heat and leave it, still covered, for another 3–4 minutes.
- Meanwhile, make the sauce. Put the garlic, ginger, yellow beans in salted sauce, chiles, and cilantro into a food processor and blend. Pour the mixture into a bowl and mix in the stock, lime juice, light soy sauce, and sugar. Now pile the rice onto the plates, carve the chicken, and arrange it on top of the rice. Serve garnished with cilantro leaves, and with the sauce in a separate bowl.
- This dish is traditionally served with Pork Ball and Tofu Soup (see page 47).

Preparation time: 20 minutes
Cooking time: 1 hour 20 minutes

Preparation time: 8 minutes
Cooking time: 5–6 minutes

stir-fried chicken with cashew nuts and baby corn

gai pad met mamuang hin ma parn

3 tablespoons oil

½ cup bite-sized pieces skinless chicken

¼ onion, sliced

6 ears baby corn, obliquely sliced

½ cup cashew nuts

½ cup light soy sauce

¼ cup Chicken Stock (see page 25)

4 teaspoons palm sugar or light muscovado or brown sugar

2 tablespoons obliquely sliced scallion

ground black pepper

1 large red chile, obliquely sliced, to garnish

○ Heat the oil in a wok and add the chicken, onion, baby corn, and cashew nuts. Stir-fry over a high heat for 3 minutes.

○ Reduce the heat and stir in the soy sauce. Then add the stock, sugar, and scallion, and season with black pepper. Raise the heat and stir-fry for another 2 minutes.

○ Transfer to a serving dish, sprinkle with sliced chile, and serve.

Preparation time: 6 minutes, plus marinating
Cooking time: 15 minutes

coconut broiled chicken

gai yarn maprow

This dish will serve 4 as part of a Thai meal, but if you plan to serve it in Western style, with rice and a salad, allow 1 chicken breast for each person.

2–3 boneless chicken breasts

Marinade:

1¾ cups coconut milk

4 garlic cloves

4 small green or red chiles

1-inch piece of fresh ginger, sliced

grated zest and juice of 1 lime

2 tablespoons palm sugar or light muscovado or brown sugar

3 tablespoons light soy sauce

1 tablespoon fish sauce

¾ cup cilantro leaves, stalk, and root

To garnish:

scallion slivers

red chile, finely diced

○ To make the marinade, blend together all the ingredients.

○ Make 3 oblique cuts on each side of the chicken breasts, place them in a dish, and pour over the marinade. Cover and leave them in the refrigerator for 2 hours.

○ Preheat the broiler and arrange the chicken pieces in the broiler pan, making sure they are fairly thickly spread with the marinade. Broil for about 15 minutes, turning occasionally. The skin side will take a little longer than the other side.

○ Meanwhile, heat the remaining marinade, adding a little of the chicken stock if it is too thick.

○ When the chicken is cooked, slice it and arrange on a serving dish.

○ Serve the chicken garnished with scallion slivers and diced chile, with the sauce in a separate bowl.

Preparation time: 12–15 minutes
Cooking time: 5 minutes

red curry duck
gaeng pet ped yaung

¼ roast duck

1 tablespoon oil

1½ tablespoons Red Curry
Paste (see page 19)

⅔ cup coconut milk

1 tablespoon palm sugar or
light muscovado or brown
sugar

3 lime leaves, torn

¼ cup peas

1 large red chile, obliquely
sliced

¼ cup Chicken Stock (see
page 25)

1½ tomatoes, quartered

1 cup pineapple chunks

1 tablespoon fish sauce

- Take the skin and meat off the duck, chop it into bite-sized pieces, and set aside.
- Heat the oil in a wok, add the red curry paste, and fry, stirring, for 30 seconds. Add 3 tablespoons of the coconut milk, blend it with the paste, then add the remainder and stir over a gentle heat for 1 minute.
- Add the duck and stir for 2 minutes. Add the sugar, lime leaves, peas, chile, chicken stock, tomatoes, and pineapple. Mix well and, with the curry simmering, add the fish sauce. Give it all a good stir, transfer the contents of the wok to a bowl and serve.

Preparation time: 20 minutes
Cooking time: 10 minutes

duck paolo
pet paolo

¼ roast duck
1 tablespoon oil
1 tablespoon chopped garlic
½ teaspoon ground black
  pepper
2 tablespoons paolo powder
2½ cups Chicken Stock (see
  page 25)
2 x 1-inch pieces
  cinnamon stick
2 star anise
2 eggs, hard-cooked and
  peeled
⅔ cup cilantro leaves, stalk, and
  root
1 teaspoon dark soy sauce
1 tablespoon palm sugar or
  light muscovado or brown
  sugar
3 tablespoons light soy sauce

○ Take the skin and meat off the duck, chop it into bite-sized pieces, and set aside.
○ Heat the oil in a wok, add the garlic and black pepper, and stir-fry until the garlic begins to turn golden. Add the paolo powder, stir well, and pour in the chicken stock. Add the cinnamon and star anise, and bring gently to a boil, stirring. Add the duck and eggs, and turn the heat down to a simmer.
○ Cut the cilantro stalk and root into small pieces, reserving the leaves. Add the stalk and root, the dark soy sauce, sugar, and light soy sauce to the wok. Stir well and allow to simmer for 3 minutes.
○ Remove the eggs with a slotted spoon and halve them.
○ Transfer the contents of the wok to a serving bowl, taking care to arrange the eggs, yolk side up, around the edge. Garnish with the reserved cilantro leaves.

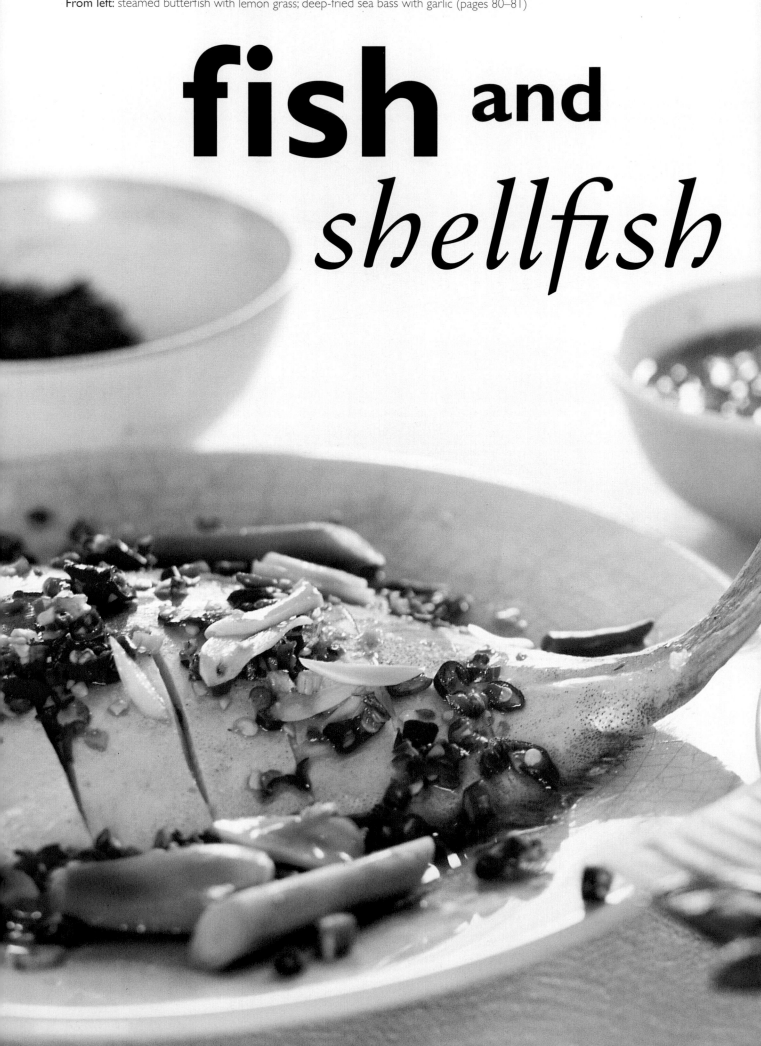

From left: steamed butterfish with lemon grass; deep-fried sea bass with garlic (pages 80–81)

fish and *shellfish*

Thailand abounds with fish and shellfish. The protein derived from them is essential, and even the very poorest people can eat rice mixed with shrimp paste and soups flavored with fish sauce. The sea is still full of fish, although not as many as there were, as are the rivers, and fish and shellfish farms are ever increasing. Southern Thailand is the region most famed for its seafood and for its use of coconut milk and flesh—coconut palms grow widely throughout the region.

Preparation time: 15–20 minutes
Cooking time: 40 minutes

deep-fried sea bass with garlic
pla kapong tod kratiem

about 3¼ cups oil,
  for deep-frying
1 x 1¼ lb whole sea bass,
  cleaned
2 tablespoons oil
15 garlic cloves, sliced
2 tablespoons palm sugar or
  light muscovado or brown
  sugar
1 tablespoon light soy sauce

Sauce:

7 small green chiles
3 garlic cloves
5 tablespoons fish sauce
3 tablespoons lime juice
1 teaspoon palm sugar or light
  muscovado or brown sugar
⅓ cup chopped cilantro leaves,
  stalk, and root

To garnish:

scallion slivers
red chiles

- Heat the oil in a wok and fry the fish for about 25 minutes. Turn it over carefully and cook for a further 10 minutes, or until really crispy. Remove the fish from the oil and drain on paper towels.
- Set the wok aside for the oil to cool, then pour off the oil and reserve to use another time.
- While the fish is cooking make the sauce. Put the chiles into a mortar and pound for 1 minute. Add the garlic and pound together for 2 minutes or until well broken down and combined with the chiles. Add the remaining sauce ingredients one by one, pounding after each addition, then pour the sauce into a bowl and set aside.
- Wipe the wok clean with paper towels.
- Put the 2 tablespoons of oil into the wok, add the garlic, and stir-fry for about 3–5 minutes, until golden and crispy. Turn off the heat and add the sugar and soy sauce, giving it a good stir.
- Place the fish on a serving dish and top with the garlic. Garnish with the scallion and chiles, and serve with the sauce.

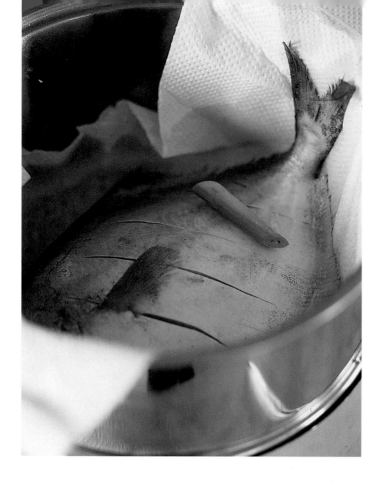

steamed butterfish

pla neung ma now

1 × 12 oz butterfish, cleaned

1 teaspoon salt

1 stalk lemon grass, cut into
  3 pieces

15 small red and green chiles

1 cilantro root, crushed and
  chopped

3 garlic cloves, finely sliced

3 tablespoons fish sauce

2 tablespoons light soy sauce

ground dried chile, to serve

- Cut oblique slashes on each side of the fish and rub the salt all over it to firm it up. Leave for 2 minutes then wash off the salt.
- Place the fish on a plate, arrange the lemon grass on top, put the plate into a steamer, and steam for 35–40 minutes.
- Meanwhile, chop the chiles very finely and put them into a small bowl with the cilantro root, garlic, fish sauce, and soy sauce, and stir thoroughly.
- To serve, pour the sauce over the fish and serve with the ground chile on the side.

Preparation time: 5 minutes
Cooking time: 35–40 minutes

Preparation time: 8 minutes
Cooking time: 12 minutes

1 tablespoon oil
1½ teaspoons Red Curry Paste
   (see page 19)
6 tablespoons coconut milk
1 lime leaf, torn
12 crab claws
⅔ cup Fish Stock (see page 25)
2 tablespoons sugar
1 teaspoon salt
⅓ cup bamboo shoots

To garnish:
½ large red chile, obliquely
   sliced
cilantro leaves

crab curry
gang pet poo

- Heat the oil in a wok, add the curry paste, and stir-fry for 30 seconds. Add all the remaining ingredients, stir well, and simmer for 10 minutes. If the liquid level reduces significantly, add more stock.
- Transfer to a bowl and serve garnished with the chile and cilantro leaves.

steamed seafood curry *hor mok talay*

8 raw shrimp, shelled but tails
   left intact
4 crab claws
3 tablespoons crab meat
2 lime leaves, finely shredded
1-inch lemon grass, finely sliced
1 egg, beaten
1 tablespoon Red Curry Paste
   (see page 19)
7 tablespoons coconut milk
¾ cup chopped Chinese leaves
⅓ cup chopped cabbage
1 teaspoon palm sugar or light
   muscovado or brown sugar
2 tablespoons fish sauce
1 large red chile, obliquely
   sliced
1¼ cups basil leaves
1 lime leaf, shredded

In Thailand this dish is usually steamed inside a young coconut. If you can buy one, cut a lid from the top and a piece from the bottom to give the coconut a flat base. Follow the recipe but put the curry into the coconut, replace the lid, and steam for 30 minutes. Then sprinkle the lime leaf on the curry, replace the lid, and steam for a further 30 minutes. Check that the curry is fully cooked—leave it to steam longer if not—and serve it from the coconut as the centerpiece of your dinner party.

- Combine all the ingredients, except the lime leaf, in a heat-proof bowl and steam, covered, for 10 minutes.
- Remove the lid, sprinkle the lime leaf on the curry, then replace the lid and steam for a further 25 minutes.

Preparation time: 10 minutes
Cooking time: 35 minutes

Preparation time: 5 minutes
Cooking time: 3–4 minutes

crab omelet
kai yat sai poo

3 tablespoons crab meat

2 eggs

1 heaping teaspoon finely
sliced scallion greens

¼ onion, chopped

3 tablespoons finely chopped
cilantro leaves

1 tablespoon fish sauce

¼ cup oil

- Combine all the ingredients, except the oil, in a bowl.
- Heat the oil in a wok until it begins to smoke. Empty the contents of the bowl into the wok and turn the heat down to low. The omelet will puff up as it cooks. After 2–3 minutes, when the underside is brown, turn it over and cook for about another 20 seconds. Gently fold the omelet in half, slide it onto a plate, and serve immediately.

hot and sour fish curry
gang som pla

5 oz firm, boneless, white fish,
such as haddock or cod

1 tablespoon Red Curry Paste
(see page 19)

1 quart Fish Stock (see
page 25)

4 ears baby corn, obliquely
sliced

1 cup chopped Chinese leaves

2 tablespoons sugar

5 tablespoons fish sauce

¼ cup tamarind water

- Poach the fish in a pan of gently simmering water for 10–15 minutes, until cooked.
- Lift the fish out of the pan and remove the skin. Put the flesh into a mortar and pound until it is soft and pulpy. Add the curry paste and mix it in well.
- Heat the stock in a saucepan, add the fish paste, and bring to a boil, stirring constantly. Reduce the heat and add the baby corn, Chinese leaves, sugar, and fish sauce, and simmer gently for 10 minutes.
- Stir in the tamarind water, simmer for 5 minutes, then serve.

Preparation time: 5 minutes
Cooking time: 30 minutes

Preparation time: 20 minutes
Cooking time: 10 minutes

thai fish cakes
tod mun pla

1 lb pollock or cod fillet,
   skinned and cut into large
   pieces
1 tablespoon Red Curry Paste
   (see page 19)
1 tablespoon fish sauce
4 lime leaves
¾ cup cilantro leaves and stalks
2 shallots, chopped
1 stalk lemon grass, sliced
2 garlic cloves, chopped
1 egg
2 teaspoons palm sugar or
   light muscovado or brown
   sugar
¾ cup peeled and finely
   chopped broccoli stalk (or
   finely sliced beans or
   chopped water chestnuts)
about 3¼ cups oil, for
   deep-frying
cilantro sprigs, to garnish
Sweet and Sour Vegetable
   Sauce (see page 117), to serve

○ Put the fish, curry paste, fish sauce, lime leaves, cilantro, shallots, lemon grass, garlic, egg, and sugar into a food processor and blend until smooth. Transfer to a bowl and stir in the broccoli.

○ Form the mixture into 16 little patties. Heat the oil in a wok, add the patties in batches, and deep-fry for about 2–3 minutes, until golden brown all over. Remove from the oil with a bamboo-handled wire basket or a slotted spoon and drain on paper towels.

○ Serve the fish cakes hot, garnished with cilantro sprigs and with the dipping sauce in a separate bowl.

chile-fried butterfish

pla lard prik

about 3¼ cups oil,
  for deep-frying
1 × 1 lb butterfish, cleaned
6 tomatoes, peeled, seeded,
  and chopped
½ cup Fish Stock (see page 25)
3 garlic cloves, chopped
3 large red chiles, chopped
2 teaspoons palm sugar or
  light muscovado or brown
  sugar

To garnish:
cilantro leaves
scallion slivers
Crispy Shallots (see page 22)

- Heat the oil in a wok. While it is heating, make oblique slashes across both sides of the fish.
- Put the fish into the hot oil and deep-fry for about 25 minutes until really crisp, turning once.
- Meanwhile, put the tomatoes, fish stock, garlic, chiles, and sugar into another wok or large saucepan. Bring to a boil, reduce the heat, and simmer, stirring occasionally, for about 10–15 minutes until the sauce has thickened and reduced.
- Remove the fish from the oil, drain on paper towels, and arrange on a plate. Pour over the sauce, garnish with cilantro, scallion, and crispy shallots, and serve.

Preparation time: 10 minutes
Cooking time: 25 minutes

stir-fried squid with basil

pla mook pad grapao

2 tablespoons oil
6 garlic cloves, chopped
12 small green chiles, finely
  sliced
1–2 shallots, chopped
4 oz squid, cleaned and cut
  into strips
½ green bell pepper, cored,
  seeded, and chopped
2 tablespoons Fish Stock (see
  page 25)
1 tablespoon fish sauce
1 teaspoon palm sugar or light
  muscovado or brown sugar
½ cup basil leaves
Crispy Shallots (see page 22),
  to garnish

- Heat the oil in a wok, add the garlic, chiles, and shallots, and fry for 30 seconds. Add the squid and green pepper, turn the heat to high, and stir-fry for 1 minute. Reduce the heat and add the stock, fish sauce, sugar, and basil. Cook, stirring, for 1 minute, then serve garnished with the crispy shallots.

Preparation time: 8 minutes
Cooking time: about 3 minutes

Preparation time: 10 minutes
Cooking time: 20 minutes

shrimp noodles
gung wun sen

⅓ cup pork belly fat

½ cup milk

1 teaspoon dark soy sauce

3 tablespoons oyster sauce

1 teaspoon chopped garlic

5 black peppercorns, crushed

⅓ cup cilantro leaves, stalk, and root

2-inch piece fresh ginger, julienned

4 oz glass noodles, soaked

12 raw shrimp, shelled, but tails left intact

2 tablespoons Fish Stock (see page 25), optional

cilantro leaves, to garnish

○ Heat the fat in a wok over a moderate heat until the oil runs, stirring occasionally. Remove from the heat and set aside. Discard the fat but leave the oil in the wok.

○ Meanwhile, combine the milk, soy sauce, and oyster sauce in a bowl.

○ When the oil has cooled down a bit—about 5 minutes—add the garlic, peppercorns, cilantro, and ginger, and stir-fry for 30 seconds. Add the noodles and the milk mixture, mix thoroughly over a high heat, then reduce the heat to low, cover the wok, and cook for 12 minutes.

○ Finally, turn up the heat, add the shrimp, and the fish stock if the sauce looks too thick, and cook, stirring, for about 2–3 minutes, until all of the shrimp have turned pink.

○ Transfer to a serving bowl and garnish with cilantro leaves.

1 tablespoon oil

½ cup finely sliced onion

1 tablespoon minced garlic

1 tablespoon ground black pepper

¾ cup peeled and sliced broccoli stalk

⅓ cup oyster mushrooms, torn

12 raw shrimp, shelled

1 teaspoon sugar

4–6 tablespoons Fish Stock (see page 25)

¼ cup light soy sauce

⅔ cup chopped cilantro leaves, to garnish

stir-fried shrimp with garlic
gung pad kratiem

○ Heat the oil in a wok, add the onion, garlic, and pepper, and stir-fry for 30 seconds. Add the broccoli stalk and stir-fry for 1 minute. Add the mushrooms and stir-fry for 30 seconds, then add the shrimp, sugar, 4 tablespoons of the stock, and the soy sauce. Stir-fry over a high heat for 1–2 minutes, adding more fish stock if the dish is drying out.

○ Serve immediately, garnished with cilantro leaves.

Preparation time: 15 minutes
Cooking time: 5 minutes

Thai people have a great love of beauty as well as food, and they often make their salads and vegetables into little works of art. Chiles and scallions are turned into leaves and tassels, root vegetables into flowers or fish. Even if you are not a fruit or vegetable carver, you can make your salads beautiful. They should always be served on a plate rather than in a bowl so that the effort that has gone into arranging them prettily can be fully appreciated. Although the following recipes are quite specific, it is fun trying different combinations, and you can add extra ingredients too, such as thinly sliced green beans, lightly cooked asparagus, shredded cucumber, blanched beansprouts, and fresh herbs.

salads and *vegetables*

duck salad
yam pet

¼ roast duck

6 small green chiles, finely sliced

½ red onion, finely sliced

⅔ cup finely chopped cilantro leaves, stalk, and root

½ tomato, cut into quarters

juice of 2 limes

1 heaping teaspoon palm sugar or light muscovado or brown sugar

1½ tablespoons fish sauce

To serve:

lettuce leaves

mint leaves

- Take the skin and meat off the duck and cut into small pieces.
- Heat a wok and then turn off the heat. Put the duck into the wok to warm it through and then add all the remaining ingredients, stirring and turning them thoroughly for 3 minutes.
- To serve, arrange the lettuce leaves and mint on one side of a serving dish and place the duck salad beside them.

watercress in garlic and oyster sauce

pad pak nam mon hoi

- Heat the oil in a wok, add the garlic, and stir-fry until golden.
- Add the watercress and stir-fry for 30 seconds, then add the oyster sauce and stock. Continue to stir-fry vigorously for 1 minute, then serve.

Preparation time: 2 minutes
Cooking time: 5 minutes

2 tablespoons oil

6 garlic cloves, finely chopped

10 oz watercress

1 tablespoon oyster sauce

2 tablespoons Vegetable Stock (see page 24)

salted egg salad
yam kai kem

10 small green and red chiles,
  finely sliced
¾ onion, sliced
⅔ cup choppd cilantro leaves,
  stalk, and root
2 tablespoons obliquely sliced
  scallion
3 tablespoons lime juice
1 teaspoon fish sauce
1 teaspoon palm sugar or light
  muscovado or brown sugar
3 Salted Eggs (see page 112),
  peeled and quartered

- Place all of the ingredients except for the eggs in a bowl and mix thoroughly for 2–3 minutes.
- Arrange the sauce on a serving dish. Add the egg quarters, turn once carefully to coat in the sauce, and serve.

Preparation time: 10 minutes

minced fish salad
yam pla duk foo

1 x 1¼ lb catfish, cleaned

12 small green chiles, finely
  sliced

½ red onion, finely sliced

⅓ cup finely chopped cilantro
  leaves, stalk, and root

3 tablespoons lime juice

3 tablespoons fish sauce

1½ tablespoons palm sugar or
  light muscovado or brown
  sugar

¼ green mango, shredded
  (optional)

1½ recipe Crushed Roasted
  Nuts (see page 24)

about 3¼ cups oil,
  for deep-frying

To garnish:

shredded white cabbage

cilantro leaves

fresh chiles

- Preheat the broiler. Place the catfish in the broiler and cook for 30 minutes, or until cooked and soft, turning once. Set aside to cool.
- Skin the fish and take off the flesh, carefully removing any bones. Mince the fish in a food processor or by hand.
- To make the sauce, put all the remaining ingredients into a bowl and mix well.
- Heat the oil in a wok until hot enough for deep-frying, then add some of the minced fish. Cook each batch of minced fish for 4–5 minutes, stirring occasionally. Remove with a slotted spoon and drain on paper towels.
- To serve, arrange the minced fish on a serving dish. Pour the sauce over the top of the fish and garnish with shredded cabbage, cilantro leaves, and chiles.

stir-fried leaf vegetables *pad pak*

2 tablespoons oil

8 cups torn mixed green
  vegetables, such as spinach,
  Chinese leaves, lettuce, and
  watercress

2 tablespoons oyster sauce

1 teaspoon palm sugar or light
  muscovado or brown sugar

2 tablespoons Vegetable Stock
  (see page 24)

2 teaspoons Garlic Oil (see
  page 22)

- Heat the oil in a wok, toss in the vegetables, and stir-fry for 30 seconds. Add the oyster sauce, sugar, and stock, and cook for about 3 minutes, stirring all the time, until the leaves have wilted.
- Transfer to a serving dish and sprinkle the garlic oil on the top.

Preparation time: 5 minutes
Cooking time: 5 minutes

Preparation time: 10–15 minutes
Cooking time: 3–4 minutes

deep-fried dried fish salad *yam pla krob*

- Pound the chiles and red onion in a mortar. Add the cilantro and pound again. Add the lime juice, fish sauce, sugar, and green mango, and pound until all of the ingredients are thoroughly mixed.
- Heat the oil in a wok and, when it is hot, throw in the small dried fish. Cook them for 2–3 minutes, until golden and crispy. Remove the fish and drain on paper towels.
- Arrange some lettuce leaves on a serving dish and place the fish on top. Pour over the sauce from the mortar and serve.

6 small green chiles, finely sliced
½ red onion, finely chopped
⅓ cup finely chopped cilantro leaves, stalk, and root
2 tablespoons lime juice
½ tablespoon fish sauce
1½ tablespoons sugar
¼ green mango, grated
about 3¼ cups oil, for deep-frying
1 cup small dried fish
lettuce leaves, to serve

Preparation time: 8 minutes
Cooking time: 1–2 minutes

squid salad
yam pla mook

½ red onion, sliced

1 tomato, cut into 8 pieces

1 tablespoon roughly chopped cilantro leaves

5 small green or red chiles, finely sliced

4 oz squid, sliced

3 tablespoons lime juice

2 teaspoons palm sugar or light muscovado or brown sugar

3 tablespoons fish sauce

5 teaspoons shredded carrot

2 tablespoons shredded white cabbage

- Place the onion, tomato, cilantro, and chiles in a mixing bowl.
- Put the squid in a saucepan of boiling water and cook for about 1½ minutes. Remove from the pot and add to the bowl.
- Add the lime juice, sugar, and fish sauce, and mix well for 1–2 minutes.
- Finally, add the carrot and cabbage, give the salad a quick stir, transfer it to a bowl, and serve.

Preparation time: 15 minutes
Cooking time: 7 minutes

warm chicken salad
laab gai

1 tablespoon oil

1 cup bite-sized pieces boneless, skinless chicken breast

1 tablespoon Chicken Stock (see page 25)

1 teaspoon palm sugar or light muscovado or brown sugar

2 tablespoons fish sauce

2 teaspoons Ground Roast Rice (see page 21)

1 stalk lemon grass, finely sliced

5 lime leaves, finely shredded

½ red onion, sliced

1 teaspoon dried chiles

½ cup cilantro leaves

mint sprigs, to garnish

- Heat the oil in a wok, add the chicken, and stir-fry over a high heat for about 4 minutes until cooked through.
- Add the stock and cook, stirring constantly, for 1 minute.
- Transfer the chicken to a bowl, stir in all the remaining ingredients, mixing thoroughly for 1–2 minutes. Serve garnished with mint sprigs.

Preparation time: 5 minutes

thai steak tartare
laab isaan

5 oz steak tartare

1 teaspoon palm sugar or light
  muscovado or brown sugar

2 tablespoons fish sauce

2 teaspoons Ground Roast
  Rice (see page 21)

1 stalk lemon grass, finely
  sliced

5 lime leaves, finely shredded

1 shallot, finely chopped

1 teaspoon dried red chiles

½ cup cilantro leaves

To serve:

lettuce

mint sprigs

tomatoes, quartered

cucumber chunks

Steak tartare is very high quality ground beef: rump steak, or fillet of course, would be ideal. Tell your butcher that you are going to make steak tartare and ask him to grind the beef finely.

- Put all the ingredients into a bowl and mix thoroughly for 2–3 minutes.
- Place the lettuce leaves on a serving dish and spoon the steak onto them. Arrange the mint sprigs on one side and the tomato and cucumber on the other.

Variation: thai fried steak tartare

- Heat 1 tablespoon of oil in a wok, add the steak, and stir-fry over a high heat for 3 minutes. Add 1 tablespoon of chicken stock and continue cooking, stirring, for 1 minute. Transfer the meat to a bowl, add the remaining ingredients, mix thoroughly for 2–3 minutes, and serve as for the main recipe.

Rice is the staple food of Thailand and is celebrated as such. In the spring the Ploughing Ceremony is held in the large open space near the Grand Palace in Bangkok in the presence of the king. This colorful ceremony, which predates the arrival of Buddhism in Thailand, is to please the gods and thereby ensure a good harvest. Rice freezes very well and can be a brilliant standby if you suddenly have unexpected guests. Fried rice should be made with cold cooked rice because the oil in which it is cooked will coat the cold grains but would be absorbed by warm grains. Noodles probably came to Thailand from China and are now totally assimilated into Thai cuisine. They are the only food that Thais eat with chopsticks.

rice and
noodles

Preparation time: 10 minutes
Cooking time: 6–7 minutes

1½ tablespoons oil

1 large garlic clove, chopped

¼ onion, chopped

½ cup chopped skinless,
  boneless chicken breast

1 egg

5 oz rice noodles, soaked

1½ tablespoons palm sugar or
  light muscovado or brown
  sugar

1 tablespoon tamarind water
  or distilled white vinegar

5 tablespoons light soy sauce

1½ cups broccoli floret and
  stalk

1 tablespoon chopped red bell
  pepper

¾ cup chopped scallion, greens
  and bulb

⅔ cup beansprouts

2 tablespoons Crushed
  Roasted Nuts (see page 24)

½ teaspoon ground black
  pepper

cilantro leaves, to garnish

fried noodles with chicken and broccoli
pad kwetio sy gai

- Heat the oil in a wok, add the garlic, onion, and chicken, and stir-fry over a high heat for 1 minute.
- Lower the heat and break the egg into the mixture, stirring constantly. Add the noodles, sugar, tamarind water, soy sauce, and broccoli, and cook, stirring, for 2 minutes.
- Add the remaining ingredients, turn up the heat, and stir-fry vigorously for about 1 minute, then transfer to a serving dish. Garnish with cilantro leaves.

fried rice *kao pad*

4 tablespoons oil

1 egg

2½ cups cold cooked rice

1 teaspoon sugar

2 tablespoons fish sauce

⅔ cup roughly chopped
  cabbage

pinch of black pepper

- Heat the oil in a wok, then break the egg into it, stirring it around and breaking it up.
- Add the rice and mix well for 2–3 minutes or until all the rice is separated. Add the sugar, fish sauce, cabbage, and pepper, and stir-fry vigorously for about 3–4 minutes, until the cabbage has wilted. Serve at once.

Preparation time: 5 minutes
Cooking time: 8 minutes

Preparation time: 10 minutes
Cooking time: 10 minutes

fried rice with pork and mushrooms

kao pad muu gup het

3 tablespoons oil

½ cup bite-sized pieces pork

1 garlic clove, chopped

1 egg

2½ cups cold cooked rice

1 tomato, cut into 8 pieces

1 teaspoon palm sugar or light muscovado or brown sugar

3 tablespoons fish sauce

1 cup sliced oyster mushrooms

2 tablespoons obliquely sliced scallion

cilantro leaves, to garnish

- Heat the oil in a wok, add the pork and garlic, and stir-fry for 2–3 minutes until they begin to turn golden. Break the egg into the wok and stir it around well. Add the rice and stir-fry for 2–3 minutes, then add the tomato and sugar, and stir-fry for 1 minute. Stir in the fish sauce, then add the mushrooms and stir-fry for 1 minute. Finally, add the scallion and mix thoroughly.
- Transfer the rice to a bowl and serve garnished with the cilantro leaves.

drunkard's noodles
pad ki mao

20 small green and red chiles
9 garlic cloves
3 tablespoons oil
½ cup ground pork
14 oz fresh Ho Fun noodles
2 tablespoons palm sugar or
   light muscovado or brown
   sugar
4 tablespoons light soy sauce
1 tablespoon dark soy sauce
1 tablespoon yellow beans
1 tablespoon oyster sauce
1 cup chopped Chinese leaves
½ cup basil leaves

○ Pound the chiles with the garlic in a mortar for about 3 minutes until all are well broken down.
○ Heat the oil in a wok, add the chiles and garlic, and stir-fry for 1 minute. Add the pork and stir-fry over a high heat for about 5 minutes.
○ Add the noodles, sugar, light and dark soy sauces, yellow beans, oyster sauces and Chinese leaves and stir-fry for 1 minute, mixing the noodles well with the other ingredients. Finally, add the basil leaves. Give it all a good stir and transfer to a serving dish.

Preparation time: 5 minutes
Cooking time: 8 minutes

noodles with gravy
kwetio lard nar gung

1 tablespoon oil
14 oz fresh Ho Fun noodles
1 tablespoon dark soy sauce

Gravy:
2 tablespoons oil
2 cups mixed green vegetables,
   such as broccoli, curly
   cabbage, sugar snap peas,
   and Chinese leaves
1 tablespoon oyster sauce
1 tablespoon yellow beans
2 tablespoons palm sugar or
   light muscovado or brown
   sugar
2½ cups Vegetable Stock (see
   page 24)
7 tablespoons light soy sauce
8–12 raw shrimp, shelled, but
   tails left intact
1 tablespoon Crispy Garlic
   (see page 22)
1 teaspoon cornflour

○ Heat 1 tablespoon of oil in a saucepan, add the noodles and the dark soy sauce, and stir for 1 minute. Remove from the heat and reserve.
○ To make the gravy, heat the oil in a wok and throw in the vegetables, oyster sauce, yellow beans, and sugar, and stir-fry for 1 minute, then add the stock and light soy sauce. Keep on stirring the boiling liquid and add the shrimp, which will turn pink in 1–2 minutes. Add the crispy garlic.
○ In a small bowl, mix the cornflour with a little water and add it to the wok to thicken the gravy.
○ To serve, transfer the noodles to a plate and ladle the gravy over them.

Preparation time: 15 minutes
Cooking time: 10 minutes

shrimp paste rice with chicken

kao kuk gabi

In Thailand, this dish is usually served with a bowl of Pork Ball and Black Fungus Soup (see page 43).

4 cups cold cooked rice

2 tablespoons oil

1 cup bite-sized pieces skinless chicken

2½ tablespoons palm sugar or light muscovado or brown sugar

3 tablespoons light soy sauce

2 tablespoons dark soy sauce

2 tablespoons Chicken Stock (see page 25)

1 tablespoon shrimp paste

½ red onion, sliced

1 zucchini, obliquely sliced

1 lime, quartered

Thai Egg Strips (see page 32), to serve

○ Reheat the rice in a steamer.

○ Meanwhile, heat the oil in a wok, add the chicken, and stir-fry for 2 minutes or until all the pieces have turned white. Add the sugar and the light and dark soy sauces, stir well, and cook for 1 minute, then add the stock and turn off the heat.

○ Put the hot rice into a bowl and stir in the shrimp paste thoroughly, so the rice begins to look a browny color.

○ Pile the rice onto plates and arrange some red onion, zucchini, and lime around the edge of each one. Reheat the chicken for 30 seconds, then pile it onto the rice. Put the egg strips on top of the chicken or serve them separately.

Preparation time: 10 minutes
Cooking time: 10 minutes

Preparation time: 3 minutes
Cooking time: 15–20 minutes

red pork rice
kao muu daeng

Traditionally, in Thailand, Red Pork Rice is eaten with Pork Ball and Tofu Soup (see page 47).

- Cut the cooked pork into slices. Cook the rice in the Thai way (see page 20).
- Put the chicken stock into the roasting pan in which you cooked the pork and heat, stirring, to deglaze.
- To serve, place the rice on a serving plate, arrange the pork on top, and pour over the juices from the roasting pan. Garnish with cilantro sprigs.

½ quantity Red Roast Pork
  (see page 58)
2 cups rice
1–2 tablespoons Chicken
  Stock (see page 25)
cilantro sprigs, to garnish

crispy noodles
mee krob

1¼ cups tamarind water
1 cup palm sugar or light
  muscovado or brown sugar
5 tablespoons ketchup
3 tablespoons fish sauce
about 3¼ cups oil,
  for deep-frying
4 oz rice vermicelli
⅓ cup of 1 x ¼-inch pieces
  ready-fried tofu
scallion tops, sliced, to garnish

- Heat the tamarind water in a wok or saucepan and melt the sugar in it—it will foam up. Add the ketchup and stir for 1 minute, then add the fish sauce. Cook, stirring, for 20–25 minutes—the sauce will gradually thicken until it is almost the consistency of jam. Remove it from the heat and allow it to cool somewhat.
- In another wok, heat the oil until it is hot enough to deep-fry the noodles, then drop them in, a handful at a time. They will puff up and expand immediately; remove them with a slotted spoon and place on paper towels to drain.
- When all the noodles are fried, put them into a large bowl and drizzle the sweet red sauce over them, working it in carefully with your hands until the crispy white noodles turn pinky-brown. Pour off all but 1 tablespoon of the oil from the wok and reserve it for another time. Arrange the noodles on a serving dish.
- Quickly fry the tofu pieces in the wok, then arrange them on top of the noodles. Sprinkle with the sliced scallion tops.

Preparation time: 6 minutes
Cooking time: 35 minutes

From left: pickled ginger; pickled garlic (page 110–111)

sauces
and *pickles*

Pickled vegetables are often served as a side dish with a meal and some are used in cooking. They are another example of the Thais love of contrasting tastes and textures. Dipping sauces perform the same function, and some form of chile hot sauce will be on the table at every meal. Egg rolls, fritters, fried fish, and raw vegetables are all served with different sauces to accompany them—sweet and hot or sour and hot, depending on your taste. *Nam Prik*—literally chile water—is the basic hot sauce, but when it is combined with pork it makes a wonderful kind of Thai spaghetti sauce. Not only is it good as a dipping sauce for raw vegetables, but it is delicious with rice or noodles too.

Preparation time: 30 minutes, plus standing
Cooking time: 10 minutes

pickled garlic
kratiem dong

6 garlic bulbs
5 cups water
1¼ cups distilled white vinegar
¼ cup granulated sugar
1 tablespoon salt

- Separate all the garlic cloves and peel them.
- Bring the water, vinegar, sugar, and salt to a boil in a saucepan, then reduce the heat and simmer for 5 minutes.
- Add the garlic to the pot, return to a boil, and boil hard for 1 minute.
- Remove the saucepan from the heat, allow the garlic mixture to cool, then transfer it into airtight containers and store in the refrigerator. Leave for 10 days before eating.

Preparation time: 2 minutes
Cooking time: 4 minutes

fresh cucumber pickle *dong tangkwa*

1 large cucumber, peeled
1 shallot, thinly sliced
5 tablespoons water
2 tablespoons granulated sugar
2½ tablespoons distilled white vinegar
pinch of dried red chile
pinch of salt

- Cut the cucumber in half lengthwise and slice the halves into ¼-inch-thick pieces. Put the cucumber and shallot in a bowl and set aside.
- Heat the water in a saucepan, add the sugar, and stir until dissolved. Remove the pot from the heat and allow it to cool a little, then add the vinegar, chile, and salt. Pour this pickling mixture over the cucumber and shallot and stir well. Cover the bowl and put it into the refrigerator until you are ready to serve. This fresh pickle will last for 4–5 days in an airtight container in the refrigerator.

Preparation time: 40 minutes, plus standing
Cooking time: 18–20 minutes

pickled ginger

6 tablespoons very thinly
  sliced fresh ginger
¼ teaspoon salt
½ cup rice vinegar
1 tablespoon superfine sugar

- Place the ginger in a bowl of cold water and leave it to stand for 30 minutes.
- Boil a saucepan of water. Remove the ginger from the bowl of cold water with a slotted spoon and drop it into the boiling water. Bring back to a brisk boil over a high heat, drain, and allow to cool.
- Spread out the ginger on a plate and sprinkle with salt. In a small saucepan, combine the vinegar and sugar, and heat until the sugar has fully dissolved. Place the ginger in a jar and pour the mixture over it, mixing thoroughly. Allow to cool, then put the top on the jar and place it in the refrigerator.
- The pickled ginger will turn very pale pink, and will be ready to use after 1 week. It will keep in the refrigerator for 3–4 months.

Preparation time: 25 minutes, plus cooling and standing
Cooking time: 15 minutes

rice water pickle

2½ quarts water

1¼ cups glutinous rice

1 mooli radish

2 carrots

12 oz Chinese leaves or cabbage

3 garlic cloves, thinly sliced

1 tablespoon thinly sliced fresh ginger

1 teaspoon black peppercorns

2 tablespoons salt

1 shallot, peeled

2 large fresh chiles (preferably red and yellow)

- Bring the water to a boil in a large saucepan, add the rice, and boil for 15 minutes. Meanwhile, peel the mooli and carrots, and slice them thinly. Cut the Chinese leaves into 1-inch slices. Pat the vegetables dry with paper towels and set them aside.
- Strain the water off the rice into a bowl, then set the water aside to cool. Discard the rice.
- Take a 2½ quart jar and fill it with layers of vegetables, sprinkling garlic, ginger, peppercorns, and salt between each layer and ending with a sprinkling of salt on top. Bury the whole shallot and the whole chiles in the middle.
- Add the cooled rice water to just cover the top layer, cover the jar with cheesecloth, and let it stand in a cool place for 4 days, making sure the level of the liquid does not drop. If it does, top it up with cold water.
- The pickle will be ready to eat after 4 days; you can put the lid on the jar and store it in the refrigerator, where the pickle will keep for several weeks.

salted eggs
kai kem

5 cups water

5½ tablespoons salt

4 eggs, in their shells

- Heat the water in a saucepan and dissolve the salt in it. Remove from the heat and allow to cool.
- When the water is cool, pour it into a jar and gently add the whole eggs. Put the lid on and allow to stand at room temperature for 15 days.
- Remove the eggs from the jar and hard-cook.

Preparation time: 10 minutes, plus cooling and standing
Cooking time: 10 minutes

soy and vinegar dipping sauce

3 tablespoons distilled white
  vinegar or Chinese rice
  vinegar
3 tablespoons dark soy sauce
1½ teaspoons superfine sugar
2 small fresh red chiles,
  finely sliced

○ Combine all the ingredients in a bowl and stir until the sugar has dissolved.

Preparation time: 5 minutes

plum sauce

5 tablespoons distilled white
  vinegar or Chinese rice
  vinegar
4 tablespoons plum jam
1 small fresh red chile, finely
  sliced

○ Put the vinegar and jam in a small saucepan and heat gently, mixing thoroughly. Remove from the heat, transfer to a small bowl, and allow to cool.
○ Add the chile before serving.

Preparation time: 5 minutes
Cooking time: 2 minutes

Preparation time: 4–5 minutes

lime and fish sauce
nam prik num bar

6 tablespoons lime juice

2 teaspoons palm sugar or light muscovado or brown sugar

½–1 teaspoon fish sauce

½ teaspoon finely chopped shallot

1 teaspoon finely chopped red chile

○ Squeeze the lime juice into a small bowl and add the sugar. Mix well until the sugar dissolves. Add the remaining ingredients and serve.

hot sweet sauce

7 tablespoons distilled white vinegar or Chinese rice vinegar

heaping ¼ cup palm sugar or light muscovado or brown sugar

¼ teaspoon salt

1 small fresh green chile, finely chopped

1 small fresh red chile, finely chopped

○ Pour the vinegar into a small saucepan and place over a gentle heat. Add the sugar and salt, and cook, stirring, until the sugar has dissolved. Remove from the heat and allow to cool.

○ Pour the sauce into a small bowl and add the chiles.

Preparation time: 5 minutes
Cooking time: 1–2 minutes

Preparation time: 3–6 minutes
Cooking time: 1½ hours

sweet sauce
saus nam tam

½ red bell pepper, with its
   seeds
¼ cup pineapple chunks
⅔ cup pineapple juice
5 cups water
1⅓ cups distilled white vinegar
2 cups granulated sugar

○ Blend the red pepper, pineapple, and pineapple juice in a food processor and pour it into a wok or saucepan. Add the water, vinegar, and sugar, give it a good stir, and cook, simmering, for 1½ hours, until the sauce has reduced and thickened.

○ The amount of sauce this makes will give you enough for your immediate use, and you can store the rest in an airtight container, at room temperature or in the refrigerator, for about 10 days.

easy sweet and sour sauce
nam gym

○ Put all the ingredients into a saucepan or wok and bring to a boil, stirring. Reduce the heat and cook, simmering, for 20 minutes, stirring occasionally.

Preparation time: 2 minutes
Cooking time: 25 minutes

3¼ cups pineapple juice
¼ cup ketchup
1 tablespoon tomato paste
5 tablespoons sugar
7 tablespoons distilled white
   vinegar

Preparation time: 5 minutes, plus cooling
Cooking time: 5 minutes

sweet and sour vegetable sauce

¼ cup distilled white vinegar

½ cup sugar

1½ tablespoons water

2 teaspoons fish sauce

¼ cup finely diced cucumber

¼ cup finely diced carrot

1 shallot, finely chopped

2 small red or green chiles, finely sliced

- Put the vinegar, sugar, and water into a small saucepan and heat gently, until the sugar dissolves. Bring to a boil and boil for 1 minute, then set the saucepan to one side and allow the liquid to cool.
- Stir the fish sauce, cucumber, carrot, shallot, and chiles into the cooled sauce, pour into a small bowl, and serve.

easy satay sauce
nam gym satay

1 tablespoon oil

2 teaspoons Red Curry Paste (see page 19)

3 tablespoons coconut milk

½ cup water

3 tablespoons palm sugar or light muscovado or brown sugar

1 cup peanuts, crushed

- Heat the oil in a wok, add the curry paste, and cook for 30 seconds, then add all the remaining ingredients. Stir well and cook over a low heat for 10–15 minutes, stirring occasionally. Add a little more water if you feel the sauce is becoming too thick. To serve, transfer the sauce into a small bowl.

Preparation time: 1 minute
Cooking time: 15–17 minutes

There are many different kinds of sweet things available in Thailand, but the usual way to finish a meal is with a large plate of mixed fruits. Generally, the more complicated and time-consuming recipes are cooked only for special occasions. Many of the little cakes and sweetmeats can be bought from the market, as can mangoes and sticky rice, during the season. I have suggested simple recipes for the most part, but you can experiment with them. Try sliced banana or whole lychees in the coconut cream custard, or use black glutinous rice, instead of white rice, with mangoes. Make pancakes using coconut milk instead of cow's milk, and rice flour instead of wheat flour; roll them up around fresh fruit and sprinkle them with palm sugar and toasted flaked coconut.

Clockwise from left: jack-fruit seeds; limeade; and coconut cream custard (pages 120–121)

desserts

coconut cream custard

sang kia maprow on

2 large eggs
¾ cup plus 1 tablespoon
   coconut milk
¾ cup palm sugar or light
   muscovado or brown sugar
¼ teaspoon salt
2 banana leaves (optional)

- Beat the eggs in a bowl and add the coconut milk and sugar. Mix well, add the salt, and mix again.
- Pour this mixture into 4 ramekins or, if you prefer, into banana-leaf bowls.
- To make banana-leaf bowls, cut 8 equal-size circles from the banana leaves and place 2 pieces together, shiny side out. Make 4 pleats opposite each other, and secure with toothpicks to form a bowl. Make 3 more bowls in the same way.
- Put the filled ramekins or banana-leaf bowls into a steamer and steam for 15–20 minutes. Serve warm, on a plate.

limeade

nam manao

If you roll the limes around quite hard on a board with your hand, you will find that you get more juice from them.

6 limes
½ cup superfine sugar
3¼ cups boiling water
pinch of salt
ice cubes
mint sprigs, to decorate

- Halve and squeeze the limes into a large pitcher. Put the squeezed halves into a heat-proof pitcher with the sugar and water. Leave to infuse for 15 minutes.
- Add the salt, give the infusion a good stir, then strain it into the jug with the lime juice. Add 6 ice cubes, cover, and refrigerate for 2 hours or until cold.
- To serve, place 3–4 ice cubes in each glass and pour the limeade over them. Decorate with a sprig of mint.

Makes 5 cups
Preparation time: 6 minutes, plus infusing and chilling

Makes about 20
Preparation time: 5 minutes, plus soaking and cooling
Cooking time: about 30 minutes

jack-fruit seeds
met kanun

- Put the beans, coconut milk, and palm sugar into a wok over a very low heat. Stir and mash constantly until the mixture blends and becomes thick and pliable like a dough. You must keep stirring and turning all the time, as the mixture burns very easily. When it has reached the correct consistency, remove it from the wok and set aside to cool.
- Put the water and superfine sugar into a wok or saucepan and boil until it becomes thick enough to make a glaze.
- Form oblong shapes about 1½–2 inches long from the cooling mixture—they are said to resemble jack-fruit seeds. Coat each one in the egg yolk, then carefully put them into the simmering sugar glaze, in batches. Roll them around in the glaze for 2 minutes, then remove with a slotted spoon and arrange on a serving dish. Make sure they do not touch each other or they will stick together.

½ cup split yellow beans,
  soaked for at least 3 hours
1¾ cups coconut milk
heaping ½ cup palm sugar or
  light muscovado or brown
  sugar
1⅓ cups water
1 cup superfine sugar
3–4 egg yolks, whisked

Preparation time: 2–3 minutes
Cooking time: 40 minutes

tapioca and young coconut
beeak sar koo maprow on

⅔ cup tapioca pearls

14 oz can of young coconut flesh or 2 cups chopped fresh young coconut flesh

¼ cup thick coconut milk

1 teaspoon palm sugar or light muscovado or brown sugar

pinch of salt

- Put the tapioca pearls into 5 cups of water and boil for 10 minutes. Drain the tapioca, cover with fresh water, and boil gently for about 30 minutes until it is cooked, occasionally topping up the liquid.
- Turn off the heat and add the young coconut flesh and its juice.
- Mix the coconut milk, sugar, and salt in a small bowl.
- Serve the dessert warm with a tablespoon of the coconut-milk mixture on each portion.

mango and sticky rice
kaoniao mamuang

2½ cups glutinous rice, soaked for at least 6 hours or overnight

¾ cup sugar

1¼ cup coconut milk

2 ripe mangoes

- Drain and rinse the rice well. Cook in a steamer for about 30 minutes. Give the rice a good shake halfway through steaming to ensure it is evenly cooked.
- While the rice is steaming, place the sugar and coconut milk in a large bowl and stir well.
- When the rice is cooked, transfer it to the coconut mixture and stir thoroughly for 2–3 minutes to achieve a rather creamy consistency. Cover with a lid and allow to stand at room temperature for 30 minutes.
- Before serving, slice the mangoes and arrange them attractively on a dish around the rice.

Preparation time: 10 minutes, plus soaking and standing
Cooking time: 30 minutes

Preparation time: 15–20 minutes

fresh fruit platter

- Peel and thickly slice the mangoes and cut the papaya into 4 or 8 pieces. Peel the lychees. Cut the watermelon into chunks, removing as many of the seeds as you can.
- Arrange the fruit on a serving plate, with the lime quarters ready to squeeze over the papaya.

2 ripe mangoes

1 small ripe papaya

8 oz lychees

1 slice watermelon

1 lime, cut into quarters

Preparation time: 2 minutes
Cooking time: 10 minutes

bananas in coconut milk

This is a very easy and simple dessert. It doesn't look particularly appealing but it tastes really good.

¾ cup plus 1 tablespoon
  coconut milk
7 tablespoons water
3 tablespoons palm sugar or
  light muscovado sugar
1 large or 2 small bananas,
  halved lengthwise and each
  half cut into 4 pieces

○ Put the coconut milk, water and sugar into a saucepan, and simmer for about 6 minutes, stirring occasionally. Add the bananas and cook for 4 minutes until heated through.

Preparation time: 5 minutes
Cooking time: 15 minutes

thai fried bananas
gluay buat chea

1¼ cups self-raising flour
½ cup water
2 teaspoons palm sugar
  or light muscovado or
  brown sugar
1 tablespoon toasted
  sesame seeds
about 3¼ cups oil,
  for deep-frying
4 bananas
3 tablespoons toasted
  desiccated coconut

○ Mix the flour, water, sugar, and sesame seeds in a bowl to make a light batter.
○ Heat the oil in a wok and, while it is heating, peel the bananas. Cut them in half lengthwise, and cut each half into 2–3 pieces. Coat the bananas thoroughly in the batter. When the oil is hot enough, carefully slide in the banana, in 2 batches, and fry for 5–7 minutes, until golden brown. Remove and drain on paper towels.
○ To serve, arrange the banana fritters on a serving plate and sprinkle with the toasted coconut.

index